MW00667257

LIVING THE
SEASONS

"Erica gives inspiration to every Catholic family to incorporate the traditions of our Catholic faith. Whether you are crafty or have limited time and a limited budget, there is something for everyone to deepen their faith by celebrating the Church's feasts and solemnities. I personally love the focus on not-so-familiar saints like St. Oscar Romero and St. Zelie Martin. Erica's relatable tone and easy how-tos make this book a go-to in my Catholic library—one I'll reach for again and again."

TABITHA KIDMAN

Owner and lead designer of House of Joppa

"As Catholics, we can forget that our faith isn't meant to be just an idea or abstract theory. But it's a living reality, one that is brought to life as we celebrate and remember all that God has done and is doing. In this inspiring and practical book, Erica Tighe Campbell provides a toolkit for incarnating the beauty of Catholic traditions into your life and family. As a dad, I can't wait to try some of these ideas with my kids to help bring the faith alive for them."

STEVE LAWSON

Founder of *Monk Manual*

"From cover to cover, this book is a delightful feast for the senses, offering creative and practical ideas for celebrating Christian seasons year-round. With five children of my own, I know firsthand the challenge of finding ways to mark special occasions in a meaningful and memorable way, but *Living the Seasons* simplifies and inspires the process. And while the book acknowledges the spiritual dimension of many celebrations, it does so in a way that is inclusive and accessible to all, regardless of religious background. Whether you're Catholic or broadly Christian, this book offers a rich and diverse array of traditions and practices that will help you connect with the rhythms of nature and the seasons and deepen your sense of gratitude and wonder. This book is bound to become my go-to resource for creating meaningful and beautiful celebrations in our home."

JEANNIE GAFFIGAN

Actress, producer, and comedy writer

"As a Catholic mom and creative who has the desire to deepen my family's faith, I can't recommend this book enough! Its stunning design and thoughtful approach to living the liturgical seasons at home are an intentional tool to transform our family's spiritual life. From creative meal ideas and crafts to meaningful reflections and prayers, every page is filled with inspiration and practical ideas that make celebrating the liturgical year a joyous and powerful experience. Wherever you are on your faith journey—from a seasoned liturgical living pro to just starting out—this book is a gift for any Catholic home."

MICHELLE BENZINGER

Cohost of the *Abiding Together* podcast

"Erica not only has an eye for beauty and creativity for miles but also an inner well of spirituality that imbues her work with depth and meaning. *Living the Seasons* is a warm, generous invitation into a celebration of faith that is sure to birth your family's most beloved traditions."

SHANNON K. EVANS

Author of *Rewilding Motherhood*

"As a busy mom of many, I am always on the hunt for resources that will make my life simpler. *Living the Seasons* does just that. This book provides a busy mom with simple and achievable ways to live liturgically at home, all with the beauty and inspired aesthetic quality Be A Heart fans know and love. Erica has crafted a book that will both inspire and equip. This book is a must-have for every Catholic mom's coffee table."

LISA CANNING
Interior designer and life coach

"If you're looking to bring more faith and meaning to your home, *Living the Seasons* is an absolute must-read! This beautiful book is jam-packed with amazing ideas and actionable tips that will leave you feeling empowered and inspired to incorporate liturgical feasts, saint stories, and holy days into your daily life in fun and creative ways. I can't wait to share it with my kids!"

ANNA LIESEMEYER
Founder and owner of In Honor of Design

"As a creative person who loves to think of ways to celebrate liturgically year-round, I am so excited that Erica has created a resource that does just that with her new book! She masterfully captures the essence of what it means to engage with the sacred in our lives, inviting us to experience the richness and beauty of our Catholic faith by living in the rhythms of our Church seasons. Through prayer, personal stories, reflections, crafts, and music, Erica invites us to embrace the seasons of the Church in a beautiful and creative way."

VALERIE DELGADO
Owner and creator of Pax.Beloved

"*Living the Seasons* unveils the beauty of incorporating the rhythms of the seasons of the Church into our lives in simple, yet profoundly meaningful, ways that draw us more intimately to the divine. As a father and musician, I believe in the importance of sharing this with my young children. My wife and I will reach for this book again and again to be inspired by the different ways that we are each called to follow God."

IKE NDOLO
Christian singer, songwriter, and recording artist

"God is more domestic than monastic. Drawing upon the joys of ordinary family life, Erica shows how God is present in every moment of our everyday lives. This book, loaded with beautiful prose and art, helps teach us what the liturgical cycle looks like in our homes."

FR. RONALD ROLHEISER, OMI
Author of *Wrestling with God*

LIVING THE SEASONS

SIMPLE WAYS TO CELEBRATE THE BEAUTY OF YOUR FAITH THROUGHOUT THE YEAR

erica Tighe Campbell

Owner and designer of Be A Heart

AVE MARIA PRESS AVE Notre Dame, Indiana

Some crafts will call for the use of a template. You can find these as a free download on the Be A Heart website or by scanning the QR code at right.

Unless otherwise noted, scripture quotations are from *New Revised Standard Version Bible*, copyright © 1989 National Council of the Churches of Christ in the United States of America. Used by permission. All rights reserved.

With contributions by Augusta D'Ambrosio.

© 2023 by Erica Tighe Campbell

All rights reserved. No part of this book may be used or reproduced in any manner whatsoever, except in the case of reprints in the context of reviews, without written permission from Ave Maria Press®, Inc., P.O. Box 428, Notre Dame, IN 46556, 1-800-282-1865.

Founded in 1865, Ave Maria Press is a ministry of the United States Province of Holy Cross.

www.avemariapress.com

Hardcover: ISBN-13 978-1-64680-231-9

Cover and text design by Brianna Dombo.

Cover and interior photographs by Hannah Hoggart.

Printed and bound in China.

Library of Congress Cataloging-in-Publication Data is available.

This book is dedicated to all the women
in our community who seek to be in communion
with God, who continue to grow more fully into
who God beckons them to be, and who in turn
bring more light and love into the world.

CONTENTS

INTRODUCTION

to every thing there is a season, and a time to every purpose under heaven.

Ecclesiastes 3:1

I've been a Catholic my whole life. I was born into a Catholic family and baptized as a young baby. One grandmother converted to Catholicism when she married my Irish Catholic grandfather, and my other grandfather converted when he married my Irish Catholic grandmother. As a family, we prayed before meals, went to Sunday Mass, and attended religious education. We marked Advent with a calendar and wreath, celebrated Christmas, observed Ash Wednesday and Lent, and feasted during Easter. Beyond that, the only feast day I knew of was for St. Francis of Assisi on October 4 because it was also my birthday and we would take our pets to receive a special blessing at our local parish. It wasn't until I moved to Brazil after college that I began to learn more about the rhythms of our Church seasons.

I didn't know Portuguese when I first arrived in Brazil, and within the first week, the religious sister who I shared a room with told me that we would be going to a *festa* that night in the city. Ready for some excitement, I was eager to leave our tiny village for the first time and attend a "party." I remember feeling very hungry as we left our village, and I was looking forward to a spread of delicious Brazilian party food. As we approached the city, it became clear to me that eating was not the first planned activity. The "party" was to be held in honor of a Catholic feast day, and that celebration would begin with a two-hour-long Mass with thousands of people in the streets of the city. The only food was the Eucharist (good for my hungry soul but less so for my hungry belly). I had never seen anything like it. Due to the utter shock and my poor language skills, I can't even tell you what feast day it was, but it was the beginning of learning about the richness of the Church seasons and how they can help us develop a rhythm of faithfulness in our own lives.

Advent, Christmas, Lent, Easter, Pentecost, and Ordinary Times impact far more than the color of vestments the priest is wearing for Mass. Living these seasons with intentionality helps ground us in faith and hope in a society that is fast-paced and ever-changing. We experience throughout the year the story of God's love for his people, and we remember the truth of who we are and why we're here.

We remember that there is a time for everything—for sorrow, for joy, for contemplation, for dancing. Then when we encounter the different seasons of our lives, we have practiced drawing closer to God through it all. We do not lose hope or fall to despair when we are in a period of suffering or spiritual drought. We do not take for granted the times of rejoicing. And we learn how to seek God in the ordinary days.

We also learn about the different saints who lived lives of virtue while also having everyday concerns like us. Their lives can inspire us to listen to how God calls each of us individually to follow him, and their witness to truth and goodness can give us courage and confidence to press on, even when all seems lost.

* * *

When I moved to Los Angeles as a young adult, I met big Catholic families who homeschooled their children and observed feast days regularly. It was beautiful, but as a single woman in my late twenties, that lifestyle didn't resonate. My curiosity was piqued, though, and I started paying more attention to the Church calendar. What I found is that living in the rhythm of the Church is not only for homeschooling moms or religious communities, as the internet might have us believe. It is for each of us, in each stage of our lives, and can be adapted to enrich our lives if only we can see how.

Eight years later, I am married with two children. My husband and I both have vibrant careers, and juggling the demands of family life leaves me feeling exhausted with little space for crafting and cooking extravagant meals. However, I see the beauty of the centuries-old traditions and the real benefits of celebrating the feast days set out in the Church calendar. I want both to live them for myself and to teach them to my daughters. I am not an expert on anything. I do not have a degree in theology, and my working memory has worsened with having children, so remembering things about saints and feast days is a bit of a challenge for me. I am one of the regular women in the pews who longs to draw close to God because my life is immeasurably better with rhythms of prayer and spiritual connection.

This book is not meant to be all-encompassing but rather a beautiful introduction to modern ways we can embrace the rhythms of the Church year. You'll find both simple activities and intricate projects to help you live the seasons, celebrate the holy days, and observe the feast days.

Let us link arms in our pursuit toward holiness.

Blessings to you,

erica tighe campbell

HOW TO USE THIS BOOK

Start Anywhere, Anytime

The Church year begins on the first day of Advent, but you can start living these traditions any time of the year. We hope this book is beautiful enough to be left out on your coffee table to be flipped through for inspiration. We did not include every feast day in these pages, but we did provide a menu of days and seasons for you to consider.

> **BEGIN WITH WHAT YOU KNOW:** Which holidays are you already celebrating? Christmas? Easter? St. Patrick's Day? Starting with what is familiar will help you feel less intimidated by all the options.
>
> **START WHERE YOU ARE:** What season is it right now? Lent? Summer? Advent? Letting the annual calendar or Church calendar choose where you start eliminates paralysis by analysis.
>
> **FIND WHAT YOU LOVE:** Who is your favorite saint, and when is their feast day? Maybe this is your Confirmation saint, or maybe it's just a saint whose story has touched you. Add their day to your calendar. You can do this for saints chosen by each member of your household. Alternatively, using this book, choose one new feast day a month to add to your calendar. Beginning with what (or who) inspires you can ensure that this remains fun and creative. Whatever your method for choosing which days, do not—I repeat, do not—try to celebrate every day mentioned in this book. You will find yourself overwhelmed, and that's the last thing we want. Use this book like a menu or a magazine—flip through it and choose what appeals to you.

For each day or season, you'll find a variety of ways to celebrate. Some activities are simple with no supplies needed. Some are more intricate than others and would excite the crafter and maker. Some are specifically for children, and some are for anyone of any age. Some are geared toward older children and adults but can be adapted for younger kids. There is something for everyone at every stage of life.

No matter where you start, be sure to start small with what already easily fits into your pace of life. Let this book be a starting point for inspiration and not a way to feel guilty for not doing enough. Living the Church seasons is an invitation to a deeper relationship with God and his promises for us by entering into the stories and history of our faith in order to more deeply contemplate and connect with God in our everyday lives. It doesn't have to be perfect or picture-worthy. It just has to be for him.

Easily Accessible Supplies

All supplies needed for crafts and meals can be found easily on Amazon or at your local craft and party stores. Some items can be purchased premade from Be A Heart (www.beaheart.com/livingtheseasons).

> Some crafts will call for the use of a template. These can be found as a free download on the Be A Heart website: https://beaheart.com/pages/living-the-seasons. To use the templates, download and print the templates, choose the pages for the craft you want to make, and cut out the shapes as instructed for the craft.

* * *

This book is nowhere near exhaustive. The Church has canonized thousands of saints throughout the centuries, and creatives have come before us and found genius ways to enliven the seasons of the Church through crafting, baking, celebrating, contemplating, and serving. We strived to make sure you have at least a handful of options for each Church season, a couple of saints or feast days per month of the year, and some essential ideas for deepening your love for God and neighbor as you move through the calendar. If you want to know more about a particular season, saint, or celebration, we've offered a list of additional resources in the appendix of this book. You will also find further reading, ideas, and resources at www.beaheart.com/livingtheseasons.

advent

MEANING: "TO COME TO"

THE FOURTH SUNDAY BEFORE CHRISTMAS
DAY THROUGH CHRISTMAS EVE

ADVENT

*The Lord is coming, always coming. When you have ears to hear and eyes to see, you
will recognize him at any moment of your life. Life is Advent; life is recognizing the
coming of the Lord.*
—Henri Nouwen

Meaning "to come to," Advent is a liturgical season that includes the four Sundays prior to Christmas. Advent is my favorite season of the year. It is the beginning of the Church year, but it can be difficult to enter into it because of the many demands placed on us during this time. Over the past few years, I have tried to become very intentional about how I live the Advent season as a time of waiting, preparation, and hope. I was at the end of my pregnancy with my first daughter, Frances, during Advent. The experience helped me connect with the pregnant Mary as she awaited the birth of her son. I wondered how she could have endured riding on a donkey with the aches and pains of the pregnant body, and I shared in the excitement of anticipating the new baby.

I began to wonder about the messages we received with holiday traditions of Santa—that if you're not "good," then you don't receive presents. It seemed to look a lot like the message I had received about God—that if I was "good" and followed the rules, then God would reward me with the things that I wanted in life. As I have grown in my spiritual life, I have come to believe that Advent is actually an opportunity to approach the manger with our failures and faults and still find ourselves loved by Christ.

Advent is a time to prepare ourselves, to orient our hearts to love both Jesus and our neighbor. It is a time to ponder things in our hearts as Mary did and sow peace in the world around us. When I was a child, I would spend days on end handcrafting Christmas cards for family and friends. I remember one year my mom let me use the glue gun to stick hay onto a construction-paper creche. I burned my fingers and damaged the wood kitchen table, but I was so proud of my creations. I handwrote meaningful messages to each person and addressed them carefully.

Now with more responsibilities as an adult, I find the weeks leading up to Christmas can feel completely overwhelming and be filled with more stress than peace and more gift-buying than prayer. Within the Advent season there are a lot of beautiful feast days to celebrate, and we can run the risk of trying to do it all and burning out. We learn from the small baby in the manger that it is less, not more, that allows the Christ child to enter our lives.

If this is your first year celebrating Advent, I suggest starting with the wreath project and skipping the other feasts for this first year. If you've had more experience with Advent, then try to build on what has been working well for you. Maybe you deepen your prayer around the wreath with songs or readings. Maybe you add in a feast day or two. Remember, we don't have to do it all (in life or in this book). Choose what brings you joy.

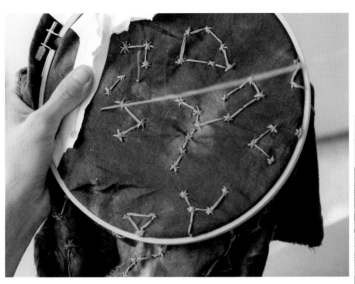

when you have
eyes to see...

EMMANUEL

SUNDAYS IN ADVENT

Light an Advent Wreath

The Advent wreath is circular as a symbol of God's unending love and eternal joy. Set out your Advent wreath and candles on your dinner table. At dinnertime starting on the first Sunday of Advent, keep the lights off or dim and light one purple candle.

Before eating, sing a verse from the hymn "O Come, O Come, Emmanuel" (pp. 6–7) and pray the following prayer. With each week of Advent, light an additional candle and experience how it becomes brighter and brighter as Christmas approaches. It is Jesus who lights up our lives!

Leader: Come, Lord Jesus, set us free.
All: Come, Lord Jesus, come.

(Light the Advent candle[s] for that week.)

Thank you, Lord, for this season of Advent
when we prepare for your arrival.
Help us to keep our eyes open
to see you when you come to us.
Bless this food, which reminds us of the banquet
we will all share with you one day in heaven. Amen.

Leader: Come, Lord Jesus, set us free.
All: Come, Lord Jesus, come.[1]

Sing "O Come, O Come, Emmanuel"

The lyrics of "O Come, O Come, Emmanuel" set the tone for the Advent season as we wait for the coming of Jesus Christ. As you sing each verse, notice how the mood of the song changes. We start as captives living in exile, tyranny, and darkness. We end the song celebrating that Emmanuel is opening up his heavenly home to us. In between, we always sing, "Rejoice!" No matter what, we rejoice because we know Jesus is coming.

How does the call to rejoice feel different to you in each week of Advent? How does it feel to rejoice, no matter what is going on in your life right now?

1. O come, O come, Emmanuel, and ransom captive
2. O come, O come, thou Lord of might, who to thy tribes, on
3. O come, thou rod of Jesse, free thine own from Satan's
4. O come, thou Dayspring from on high, and cheer us by thy
5. O come, thou Key of David, come and open wide our

Israel, that mourns in lonely exile here,
Sinai's height, in ancient times didst give the law
• tyranny; from depths of hell thy people save,
drawing nigh; disperse the gloomy clouds of night,
heav'nly home; make safe the way that leads on high,

Refrain

until the Son of God appear.
in cloud and majesty and awe.
• and give them vict'ry o'er the grave. Rejoice! Rejoice!
and death's dark shadows put to flight.
and close the path to misery.

Emmanuel shall come to thee, O Israel.

WEEK ONE OF ADVENT

THIS WEEK WE FOCUS ON HOPE.

Light one of the purple candles, called the prophecy candle, which symbolizes the prophets who told of Jesus's coming with anticipation.

Make an Advent Banner

* "Advent Banner" template
* Cotton canvas, 1 yard
* Fabric scissors
* Felt, colors of choice
* Iron-on hem tape (optional)
* Felt glue

Cut the cotton canvas to be 4 inches x 1 yard (if you want to hem it, give yourself an extra inch on all sides). Cut out a triangle from each end to make your banner. Hem with iron-on tape (optional). Use the template to cut out the letters from your felt; alternatively, freehand trace 3-inch-tall letters onto the felt. Use the felt glue to glue your letters onto the banner. To make sure it's centered, glue the center letters first (the center is between the *O* and *M* on the second *come*) and then move out to either side.

Now you can hang the banner on your tree, on your mantel, or in your kitchen!

Reach Out

Reach out to a friend who you know is going through a difficult time. Listen to them and support them however they might need as a sign of hope that there is light coming.

WEEK TWO OF ADVENT

THIS WEEK WE FOCUS ON PEACE.

Light two of the purple candles. The second purple candle is called the Bethlehem candle, which symbolizes the Holy Family's experience in Bethlehem.

Throw a Baby Shower for Mary

Throwing a baby shower for Mary with your friends is a fun alternative to a Christmas party. Ask guests to bring donations for a pregnancy center in your area as a gift for Mary and baby Jesus.

Create a Virgin (Mary) Mom-osa Bar

* Sparkling lemonade
* Orange juice
* Fresh fruit, especially strawberries

Strawberries grow alongside their white flowers. Because of this, they symbolize fruitful purity and have come to represent the pure, virgin mother who bears the fruit—Christ—in her womb. Add some to your mimosa to honor Mary!

Serve Mini Food

* Pigs in a blanket (they look like a baby swaddled)
* Mini pancakes and waffles
* Mini pizzas
* Mini quiche

Mary is having a BABY!

Join us to celebrate the birth of Jesus!

DECEMBER 10

RSVP December 1

Decorate Swaddle Blankets

* "Swaddle Stamps" template
* Blank white muslin swaddle blankets or burp cloths
* Fabric paint
* Foam brushes
* Pieces of scrap cardboard
* Craft foam with adhesive backing
* Scissors or X-Acto knife

Prepare a swaddle decorating station. First, make the stamps. Cut your desired shapes from the craft foam using the printed template, then adhere to small pieces of cardboard so you can easily use the stamp. Place larger cardboard pieces under the blankets so that the paint doesn't stain the table.

Apply fabric paint to the stamps with foam brushes, then decorate the swaddle blankets with the stamps. (Limit the color choices of paint so that they look a little more polished.) Hang on a clothesline to dry. You can donate these to the pregnancy center, too!

Make Space for Prayer

It can be difficult to carve out time for quiet prayer in this season. Give your guests the gift of prayer. You could provide them with a journal and pen or have them bring their own. You can also pass out an Advent reflection if you wish.

WEEK THREE OF ADVENT GAUDETE SUNDAY

THIS WEEK WE FOCUS ON JOY.

Light two of the purple candles and the pink candle. The pink candle is called the Shepherd's candle, which symbolizes the joy of meeting the Christ child.

Go to Confession

St. John the Baptist encourages us to prepare the way of the Lord by repenting and changing our lives. On Christmas Day, we want Jesus to find our hearts swept clean and ready for him.

Wear Pink

When we wear pink on Gaudete Sunday, we're celebrating a shift in the Advent season from a focus on penance and preparation to one of joy and anticipation. Wear pink to celebrate the coming Christ child!

Make a Christmas Bell Garland

Bells are rung at churches on Christmas Eve at midnight to announce the joy of the Lord. Prepare in anticipation by making and hanging a bell garland.

* Christmas bells (sometimes called cow bells)
* Linen ribbon or macrame jute

Every 12 inches along your ribbon or jute, tie on a bell with a knot. Intertwine your bell garland with greenery on your mantel, above a kitchen window, or along a staircase. Alternatively, you could hang a few strung bells on doorknobs around your house.

Visit a Nursing Home

Visit a nursing home in your area and ask if you can spend time with the residents who might not have many visitors. You can bring activities to do or just sit and listen. Ask if you can hold their hand while they talk as physical touch can do wonders for the soul.

WEEK FOUR OF ADVENT

THIS WEEK WE FOCUS ON LOVE.

Light all four of the candles. The last purple candle is called the Angel's candle, which symbolizes God's endless love—God sent angels four different times to prepare people for Jesus.

Make a Christmas Tree Angel

* Spun cotton ball
* Paper-mache cone
* Pipe cleaner
* Colorful felt sheets
* Felting wool (optional)
* Small felt balls of various colors
* Craft paint
* Paintbrush
* Felt glue
* Glue gun
* Hot glue
* Scissors

Start by painting the angel's face on the spun cotton ball. Keep the face simple. You can paint on the hair or attach wool to the head. Cut off the top of your paper-mache cone so that it is flat and a good base for your spun cotton ball head. Hot-glue the ball onto the top and let cool. Then glue on a felt sheet to the cone as the dress. Wrap your pipe cleaner around the back of the cone where the shoulders might be, and hot-glue in place to create two arms.

Wrap felting wool or scraps of felt sheet around the torso to create a shirt and around the pipe cleaner arms to create sleeves. We made little mittens to cover the ends of the arms. Use felt glue to glue on the felt pom-poms on the dress. Now she's ready to be placed on top of your Christmas tree.

ST. ANDREW

NOVEMBER 30

Born circa AD 5 in Bethsaida, Roman Empire
Died circa AD 70 in Patras, Roman Empire

PATRON SAINT OF: Fishmongers, rope-makers, textile workers, singers, miners, pregnant women, butchers, farm workers, protection against sore thoughts, protection against convulsions, protection against fever, protection against whooping cough

Pray the Christmas Novena

The St. Andrew Novena is also known as the "Christmas Novena" or the "Christmas Anticipation Prayer." It is traditionally prayed fifteen times every day from the Feast of St. Andrew the apostle until Christmas, but even praying it once each day will help keep your mind focused on the coming of Jesus.

Through praying this novena, we place ourselves mentally and spiritually in the stable where Jesus was born. It's tradition to ask God for a desire of your heart while praying this. You can download a printable on our website.

Hail and blessed be the hour and moment in which the Son of God was born of the most pure Virgin Mary, at midnight, in Bethlehem, in the piercing cold. In that hour vouchsafe, I beseech thee, O my God, to hear my prayer and grant my desires (state them here) through the merits of Our Savior Jesus Christ, and of his blessed Mother. Amen.

ST. NICHOLAS

DECEMBER 6

Born circa 270 in Patara, Roman Empire
(present-day Gelemiş, Turkey)
Died circa 343 in Myra, Roman Empire
(present-day Demre, Turkey)

PATRON SAINT OF: Children, travelers, the falsely accused, repentant thieves, unmarried people, brewers, sailors, fishers, merchants, broadcasters, pharmacists, archers, pawnbrokers, coopers

In honor of St. Nicholas's generosity, and our faith in God's promise to give good gifts to his children, we celebrate with shoes, stockings, oranges, and treats.

Set Out Shoes and Fill with Treats

Have everyone who lives in your house set out their shoes by the fireplace or the door the night before December 6. If you have children, they can set out carrots for St. Nick's horse. After they have gone to bed, fill their shoes with traditional treats: chocolate gold coins, candy canes (to represent his shepherd's staff), oranges, notes of affirmation, pictures of their favorite people, a new book, or even tools and supplies to make gifts for others.

St. Nicholas gave the gift of gold to a family in need anonymously without any expectation of receiving something in return. Over time, in keeping the St. Nicholas Day tradition of putting treats in shoes, people used oranges to represent the gold because it was costly and a fruit only available to the affluent. Oranges are now a symbol of charity (and because they are naturally segmented, they are a perfect way to discuss sharing with others).

Make Orange Surprise Balls

* Hollow plastic balls that open
* Small treats or affirmation notes
* Gold coins (optional)
* Orange crepe paper
* Green paper or felt for leaves
* Tape
* Scissors

Fill a plastic ball with small treats or an affirmation note. Cut the crepe paper into ½-inch strips and wrap around the ball. You can also hide gold coins or other small things in between the layers to make it bigger. Tape it closed. Cut leaf shapes out of green paper or felt and tape on top. Place the surprise balls inside shoes or stockings on the Feast of St. Nicholas.

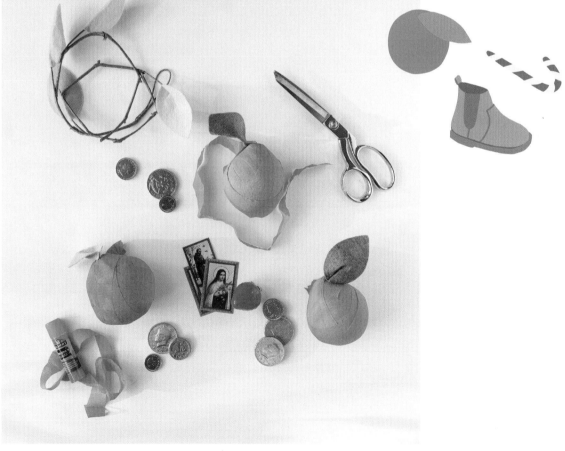

Make a Dried Orange Garland

In some churches, there is a special blessing of the oranges, after which everyone can take some blessed fruit home. You can easily do this blessing at home and then turn the oranges into a beautiful garland to decorate your mantel or staircase.

Loving God, you ask us to care for those who are in a time of need. Bless these oranges that they might be a reminder to us to be like your servant St. Nicholas and to give without seeking anything in return—especially notoriety. We ask that you turn our hearts to be of service to others and to hear the cry of the poor. Amen.

* Oranges
* Cutting knife
* Cutting board
* Paper towels
* Baking sheet
* Parchment paper
* Fishing line

Preheat your oven to its lowest possible setting, usually 150°F to 225°F (you don't want to burn your oranges). Line your baking sheet with parchment paper. Slice the oranges into thin rounds and blot them dry with paper towels. Bake for 2 to 3 hours, flipping them halfway through. They are done when they are slightly browned.

Once they cool, string them on fishing line about 2 inches apart. You can hang them around your house for a reminder all season of the spirit of giving like St. Nicholas.

Hang Candy Canes

Candy canes were originally made to represent the shepherd's staff (or crozier) of St. Nicholas. All bishops carry staffs, hooked at the top like a shepherd's crook, showing they are the spiritual shepherds who care for their people, just as Jesus is the Good Shepherd.

Simply gather the candy canes in your house or make cute candy-cane ornaments and pray a blessing over them. Hang them in special places around the house or on your tree if you have one.

BLESSING FOR CANDY CANES

Come, great-hearted saint,
and be our patron and companion
as we, once again, prepare our homes and hearts
for the great Feast of Christmas,
the birth of the Eternal Blessing, Jesus Christ.
May these sweets, these candy canes,
be a sign of Advent joy for us.
May these candy canes,
shaped just like your Bishop's staff,
be for us a sign of your benevolent care.[2]

Give to Someone in Need

St. Nicholas anonymously gave to a family in need. You can give to those in need, too.

* Donate to an organization that aids impoverished people.
* Go through a room or two in your house to find things that are still in good condition that you don't use or need. Donate them to a local charity that gives out items for free.
* Find a family to adopt for Christmas.

THE SOLEMNITY OF THE IMMACULATE CONCEPTION

DECEMBER 8

It is easy to confuse this feast with the celebration of the conception of Jesus in Mary's womb, but that feast—the Annunciation—falls nine months before Christmas, on March 25. Instead, today's feast is about *Mary's* conception. From her first moments in the womb of her mother, St. Anne, Mary was preserved from all stain of sin to prepare her to bear God's Son to the world. The Solemnity of the Immaculate Conception is a holy day of obligation.

Attend Mass

Attend Mass because it is a holy day of obligation.

Make a Rosary Accordion Box

Make and decorate this box as a special place to store your rosary. When you open it, you'll find the rosary mystery and prayers written out for reference. This makes a great gift for people who are new to the Rosary or who want a visual reminder to pray it regularly.

* "Rosary Accordion Box" template
* Jewelry gift box, 3½ x 2 inches
* Computer paper
* Glue or tape
* Scissors
* Washi tape, paint and brushes, or collage items (to decorate)

Cut the printer paper into 2-inch by 1½-inch strips. Fold and score, accordion-style, to create 8 "pages." Cut out rosary mystery and prayer pages from the template and glue them onto the accordion pages. (Alternatively, write them out by hand.) Glue the ends of the strip, prayers facing up, into the insides of the jewelry gift box. Decorate the outside of the box with washi tape, paint, or collage items.

Clean Your House

It was in the walls of Mary's house that the angel Gabriel appeared to Mary and declared her to be full of grace. Clean something in your house that you have been neglecting, and meditate on Mary's pure heart.

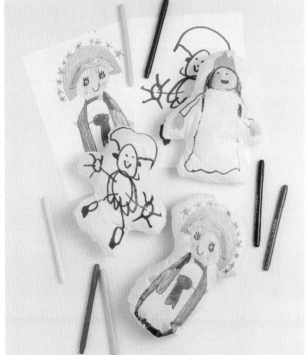

Make a Mary Pillow

* White fabric
* Fabric markers
* Fabric scissors
* Thread
* Needle
* Stuffing

Draw (or have your child draw) a picture of Mary with fabric markers onto fabric. Lay it face up on another piece of fabric and cut out the picture of Mary. Place the bottom layer of fabric on top, so that the drawing is inside, then sew around the edges to make a little pillow, leaving a 2-inch gap. Turn right-side out with the image showing, fill with stuffing, and sew the gap closed.

ST. JUAN DIEGO CUAUHTLATOATZIN

DECEMBER 9

Born 1474 in Cuauhtitlán, Aztec Empire
(modern-day Mexico)
Died 1548 in Tepeyac, New Spain
(modern-day Mexico)

PATRON SAINT OF: Indigenous peoples of the Americas

Make Guacamole

St. Juan Diego was an Indigenous Nahua; and guacamole originates from his people. Make (or buy!) guacamole to serve with a meal. Enjoy with locally made tamales.

Make Rose Ink

* Petals from 1 rose
* 1 cup water
* A dash of salt
* 1 teaspoon white vinegar
* Gum arabic
* Wintergreen oil
* Small saucepan (preferably old)
* Bowl
* Ladle
* Coffee filter
* Funnel
* Glass bottle for ink

In an old saucepan, add the rose petals, water, salt, and white vinegar. Heat the mixture for at least an hour, keeping just below boiling. Place a coffee-filter-lined funnel into a bowl. Carefully ladle the liquid into the funnel, and discard any rose petals or solids caught in the filter. While the liquid is still hot, add to the bowl gum arabic at a ratio of 2½ teaspoons per ½ cup of ink. Add a drop of wintergreen oil to a glass bottle and then pour your ink into the bottle. Mix well. Use the ink like watercolor paint!

OUR LADY OF GUADALUPE

DECEMBER 12

Our Lady of Guadalupe is a title for Mary that came from an apparition that took place in present-day Mexico. She appeared three times to fifty-seven-year-old Indigenous Nahua St. Juan Diego in 1531.

Embroider a Constellation Prayer Table Cover

The forty-six stars on Mary's mantle are in the exact layout of the night sky over the place she appeared to Juan Diego in Mexico on December 12, 1531.

* "Constellation Prayer Table Cover" template
* Teal or blue fabric, 12 x 18 inches
* Pins
* Embroidery hoop
* Gold embroidery thread
* Embroidery needle
* Scissors

Secure the template on the fabric with pins. Place the fabric on the inner hoop, then place the outer hoop on top. Tighten the screw, gently tugging the edges of the fabric and paper if needed, until the fabric is stable and taut. You will be sewing through the fabric and template paper at the same time.

To embroider, cut a piece of embroidery thread the length of your arm. Tie a knot a few inches from one end, then pull 4–6 inches of the other end through the needle. From the underside of the hoop, insert the needle into the start of a constellation on the template and pull through until the knot catches on the fabric. Put the needle down at the end of the line, and pull. Make little stars over the dots by crisscrossing 3 or 4 lines over the dots, as shown in the photos at right. Repeat these sewing steps until you've completed the constellation. You can tear away the template paper after you finish each section.

The fabric can be used on your prayer table or hung on the wall.

Decorate with Roses

Roses were not in season when Mary appeared to Juan Diego, but they were miraculously blooming on the hill where he met her. She instructed him to put them in his cloak and take them to the local bishop to prove the apparition. When he dropped the roses at the bishop's feet, the image of Our Lady of Guadalupe appeared on his tilma. Decorate with roses to brighten your home during this wintry Advent season, as a way to remember the hope Our Lady of Guadalupe brings to all people through her son.

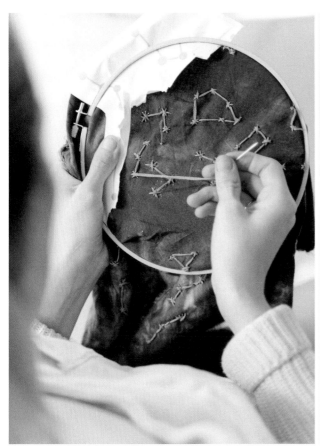

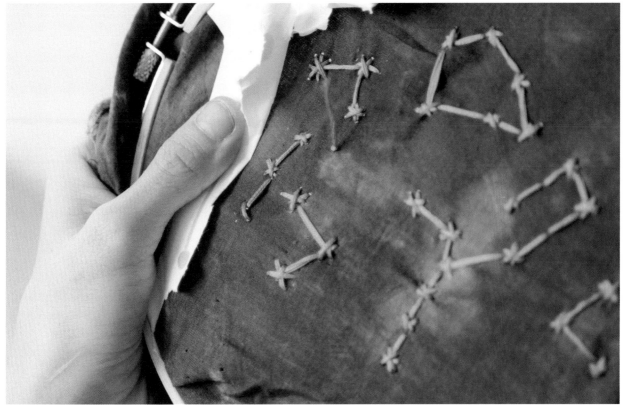

ST. LUCY

DECEMBER 13

Born circa 283 in Syracuse, Roman Empire
(present-day Italy)
Died circa 304 in Syracuse, Roman Empire
(present-day Italy)

PATRON SAINT OF: Martyrs, the blind, epidemics, writers

Lucy is a name that comes from the Latin word for "light." Lucia is an Italian saint from the ancient city of Syracuse known for her bravery in defending her faith at a young age. She is celebrated throughout the world on one of the darkest and coldest days of the year, as a symbol that Christ can light up even the darkest places.

Plant Christmas Wheat

In Hungary, people plant wheat on St. Lucy's feast day and care for it daily until Christmas; by then a green shoot will be several inches tall.

* Shallow round pot
* Acrylic paint (optional)
* Paintbrush (optional)
* Wheat grains
* Soil

Paint the pot if you want. When dry, fill it with soil. Place the wheat grains in the soil and press them lightly to be just under the surface. Keep the pot indoors in a warm room, and water it daily. Keep the soil damp but not soggy. As a symbol of new life and the Eucharist, the green shoot reminds us of the infant Jesus in the manger.

Bake Santa Lucia Buns

Make Santa Lucia buns the night before (or any sweet pastries!). In the morning, the eldest daughter of the family wears a white nightgown and passes them out to every family member!

Use No Electricity after Dark

St. Lucy was from Italy, so no one is certain how the legend of Santa Lucia made it to Sweden. It is believed that Lucia and her feast day were adopted as a way to let in some light at the beginning of the dark, cold Swedish winter. December 13 was thought to be one of the coldest and darkest days of the year.

Do not use any electricity after dark. Turn off all the lights and only use candles for light. Use the time for prayer and meditation, and maybe get some extra sleep.

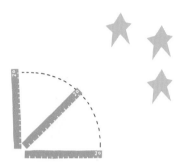

Make St. Lucy's Day Headwear

Make a Santa Lucia Crown (for Girls)

* Vintage wooden clothespins
* White spray paint
* Glue gun
* Hot glue
* Cardboard box or molding foam
* Acrylic paint in oranges and yellows
* Paintbrush
* Artificial garland
* Wire wreath base, or wire formed into a sturdy oval

Spray-paint the clothespins white. Use the glue gun to create faux wax "drips" on the sides of the clothespins. Then spray-paint white again. Cut out teardrop shapes from the cardboard (I ended up using molding foam rather than cardboard) and paint them yellow and orange to make little flames. Then hot-glue a flame to the top of each clothespin.

Drape the artificial garland over the wreath base to make a wreath crown, and secure with hot glue. Then clip the clothespin candles onto the crown.

Make a Star Boy Hat (for Boys)

* "Star Boy Hat" template
* White poster board or heavy paper, at least 22 x 28 inches
* Pencil
* Scissors
* Yellow or gold paper or felt
* Elastic band or ribbon to tie
* Glue
* Hole punch

On the poster board, mark a small dot in the middle of one long edge and a dot in one of the opposite corners. Draw an arched line between the dots. Cut along the line; this will be the bottom edge of the cone. Roll the paper into a cone, and glue along the connecting edges. Use the template to cut 2 stars out of the paper or felt, and glue onto the cone. Hole-punch opposite sides of the cone near the bottom. String an elastic band or ribbon through the holes to make a tie.

O ANTIPHONS

DECEMBER 17–23

The O Antiphons are an ancient part of the Church's evening prayer as we approach Christmas. An antiphon is simply a verse or line that is used as a refrain during prayer, and each of these begin with the exclamation "O" and capture a different title for Jesus.

By reciting these, traditionally in the octave (eight days) before Christmas, we pray for Christ to come fulfill not only Old Testament hopes of the Messiah but our present hopes as well. We pray for light in the darkness. We all experience, individually and collectively, loneliness, longing, hopelessness, and expectation. We pray for the long-expected Jesus to come into our hearts and lives and bring redemption, resurrection, and transformation.

Selected verses from the seven antiphons were compiled into the hymn we today call "O Come, O Come, Emmanuel."

In the evening (perhaps before dinner), light the Advent candles. Sing "O Come, O Come, Emmanuel" (p. 7). Then pray the O Antiphon for the day, recite the Canticle of Mary (see Magnificat on p. 152), and close with the O Antiphon again.

In ancient monasteries, the order would assign a monk to each day of the O Antiphons, and he brought a surprise for each person at the dinner table. You could incorporate this tradition into your home, workplace, or small group by assigning each member of the group a different O Antiphon. When it is their O Antiphon day, they can give a gift to each person in the group.

December 17

O Wisdom of our God Most High,
guiding creation with power and love:
come to teach us the path of knowledge!

SPECIAL TREAT: Give them something they would be interested in learning or a book that relates to something they love (knowledge).

December 18

O Leader of the House of Israel,
giver of the Law to Moses on Sinai:
come to rescue us with your mighty power!

SPECIAL TREAT: Make gingerbread houses (house of Israel).

December 19

O Root of Jesse's stem,
sign of God's love for all his people:
come to save us without delay!

SPECIAL TREAT: Put a flower stem at each place setting (Jesse's stem).

December 20

O Key of David,
opening the gates of God's eternal kingdom:
come and free the prisoners of darkness!

SPECIAL TREAT: Create a cryptogram puzzle by providing a key
(1=a, 2=b, etc.), and let them decipher the message (key) or get fun flashlights
or reading lights (key of David).

December 21

O Radiant Dawn,
splendor of eternal light, sun of justice:
come and shine on those who dwell in darkness and in the
shadow of death.

SPECIAL TREAT: Serve sunny-side-up eggs (sun of justice).

December 22

O King of all nations and keystone of the Church:
come and save us, whom you formed from the dust!

SPECIAL TREAT: Incorporate a sprinkle of cinnamon into your dessert
(signifying dust) or hot cocoa.

December 23

O Emmanuel, our King and Giver of Law:
come to save us, Lord our God!

SPECIAL TREAT: Wear paper crowns (king).

CHRISTMAS EVE

DECEMBER 24

On Christmas Eve, we await the coming of Christ. Mary is laboring to give birth to Emmanuel, a name that means "God with Us."

Decorate Your Christmas Tree Together as a Family

If you've managed to keep the tree undecorated, decorate it as a family today! You could even go pick out the tree at a Christmas tree lot today. Drink hot cocoa and spend time together.

NOEL

christmas

A CELEBRATION OF THE BIRTH OF CHRIST

SUNDOWN CHRISTMAS EVE THROUGH
THE BAPTISM OF OUR LORD

CHRISTMAS

May the Child Jesus be the star that guides you
through the desert of your present life.
—Padre Pio

God chose to become human as a helpless infant born into a family situation that was atypical. Jesus is not afraid to enter unsavory places, and he shines brightly in the darkness. He is already with me in the shameful places of my own heart and shines light into any dark crevices.

We can easily spend far too much time trying to make our homes and families picture-perfect. In Christmas letters and on social media, we end up omitting the times of suffering we experience. We build up expectations around what Christmas will bring, and we forget about the dysfunctions of our families, the grief we experience in missing loved ones we have lost, the loneliness of not having a partner, or whatever it is that causes despair in our lives. So when the day is over and the wrapping paper has to be cleaned up from the floor, there can be a feeling of disappointment. Maybe we're sad it's over, or we feel disenchanted that it didn't meet our expectations.

But the good news is that Christmas is an entire season—not just one day! I, like many people, used to think the song about the twelve days of Christmas was talking about the twelve days *prior* to Christmas—like a countdown to the big day. However, it is actually about the first twelve days of the Christmas season, which begins on December 25! The way to combat the post–Christmas Day blues is to keep celebrating!

Some families like to save presents to give one gift a day until the Epiphany on January 6. Others like to do a special family activity each day, like going to the zoo, volunteering at a soup kitchen, or having a game night. When I lived in Brazil, we each drew a name on Christmas Eve and then for the next twelve days did something kind for our person without them finding out. Then on Epiphany, we gave a bigger gift and revealed ourselves as the giver. It was so fun to focus on someone else, and it kept the spirit of Christmas alive.

The Christmas season officially ends on the Feast of the Baptism of the Lord, although historically it lasted until Candlemas on February 2. As a parent now, I appreciate that I can leave up Christmas decorations for the entire month of January.

May we spend the Christmas season contemplating how God revealed himself to us through the meekness of a child.

the star that
guides you...

CHRISTMAS DAY

DECEMBER 25

Be Completely Present in the Moment

Just as Mary and Joseph were completely present with their newborn son, turn off your phone and be with those around you. If you know of someone spending the day alone, either invite them over to join you or take a moment to go visit them.

Set Up Your Nativity Scene

St. Francis of Assisi was the first to create a nativity scene, which is now a well-known way to honor the birth of Jesus at Christmastime. If you don't already own a nativity scene, try checking thrift stores or estate sales. I have quite the collection now, all found secondhand.

Pause and reflect on the mystery of God incarnate. He who rules the universe took on human form out of love for us. The King of kings lies in a manger while Mary and Joseph look on in perfect adoration.

FEAST OF THE HOLY FAMILY

DECEMBER 30

This feast honors Jesus, Mary, and Joseph as the holiest of families and a model for all Christian families, showing us how we should all love one another as the Body of Christ.

Be Present with Your Family

Spend the day being completely present with your family or chosen family—technology-free and work-free. Focus on play, presence, and rest.

Aid Refugees

The Holy Family fled to Egypt and traced the journey that many refugees have traveled. Find an organization that aids refugees in your community. Ask what their needs are and see how you could be of service to them—either by donating goods, money, or time.

Pray for Your Family

Take a moment to pray intentionally for your family. Ask Jesus, Mary, and Joseph to watch over each of your specific needs.

If you are married, today is a good day to sit together and reflect on the last year. Where did you grow? What were your greatest delights of the year? What were the hardest things you experienced? Where did you see God moving?

What dreams do you have for the coming year? What areas do you need to discern for your family? Make a list of everything big and small, and then say a prayer together to ask the Holy Family to guide you always closer to God.

MARY, MOTHER OF GOD

JANUARY 1

This solemnity is dedicated to Mary's motherhood: to Jesus and to each of us. The Solemnity of Mary, Mother of God is a holy day of obligation.

Attend Mass

Attend Mass on this holy day of obligation.

Ring in the New Year with Mary

The title "Mother of God" comes from the Greek *Theotokos*, which means "God-bearer." We are each called to be God-bearers in this world in how we act and live. Because the solemnity lands on New Year's Day, many people choose to go to Mass for the holy day the night before on New Year's Eve. So why not throw a Marian-themed New Year's party?

Serve Marian Foods

* **Elderflower Rose Gimlet:** Roses symbolize Mary because of their beauty.
* **Pear and Gorgonzola Pizza:** Pears are an ancient symbol of Mary because of their sweetness.
* **Strawberry Rhubarb Galette:** Strawberries symbolize the fruitfulness of Mary.

Make Star and Moon Confetti Poppers

* "Star and Moon Confetti Poppers" template
* Tubes (such as toilet paper rolls)
* 9-inch balloons
* Star and moon confetti, tissue paper confetti, or pom-poms (for easier cleanup)
* Tissue paper
* Glue
* Cardstock cut to 5¼ x 3⅞ inches

Knot the end of a balloon and cut off the top before stretching it tightly over a tube. Fill with confetti. Seal the tube by gluing tissue paper over the open end. To decorate the outside of the popper, print the template on cardstock and cut to size. Decorate it and then glue it around the outside of the popper. Repeat for as many poppers as desired. To pop the confetti poppers, just pull back on the balloon and release!

Decorate with Gold Stars

Decorate the party room with gold stars to celebrate our Holy Mother and the New Year. You can find lots of options online or at a party store that will fit your space. You can also cut them out of gold poster board.

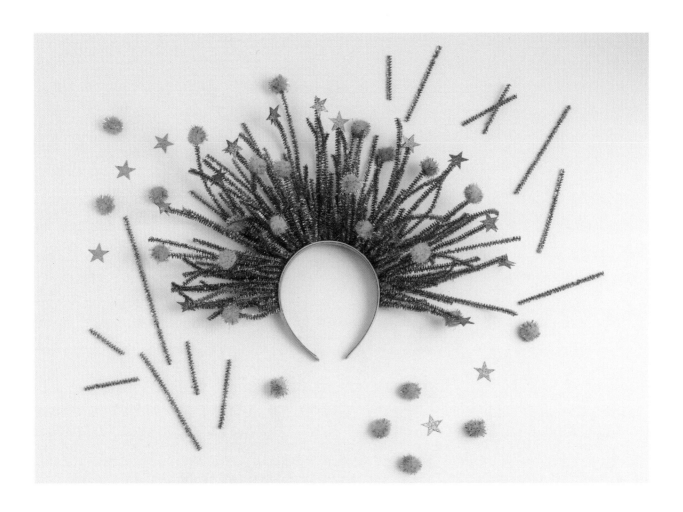

Make a Marian Halo

Mary has a crown of twelve stars, which represent both the twelve patriarchs of the tribes of Israel (original people of God) and the twelve apostles. You can pull out your crown to wear on the many Marian feast days throughout the year. This is a fun party activity if you have multiple glue guns.

* Headband
* Gold and silver pipe cleaners
* Gold pom-poms
* 12 gold stars
* Glue gun
* Hot glue
* Scissors

Glue 12 pom-poms on top of a headband as the base. Fold the pipe cleaners at various lengths and run your fingers over them to give a slight curl. In between each of the pom-poms on the headband, dab some hot glue and stick in the folded end of a pipe cleaner. Cut the pipe cleaners to your desired height, saving the offcuts for later. It will begin to take shape.

Then glue all of the offcuts in between the pom-poms and pipe cleaners. Keep going until it is nice and full. Then glue your 12 gold stars on the ends of the long pipe cleaners. You can fill in with more pom-poms on the ends of other pipe cleaners to make the crown fluffier.

Choose a Word and Saint of the Year

Prep two bowls of little papers—one bowl should have an assortment of "words" of intention, and one bowl should have an assortment of saints (see lists below). Have each guest prayerfully pick one of each. Then go around in a circle and share each person's word of the year and saint. It is also fun if you give everyone a few minutes to research their saint to share something about them with the group.

You could also add a verse of the year and write out Bible verses for people to choose from a third bowl.

Create collages using magazines with images and words based on the themes around your word and saint to hang in a prominent place at home.

A LIST OF SAINTS TO GET YOU STARTED

St. Agnes	St. Elizabeth Ann Seton	St. Michael
St. Ambrose	St. Francis de Sales	St. Óscar Romero
St. Ann	St. Ignatius	St. Paul
St. Anthony of Padua	St. Isidore the Farmer	St. Philip Neri
St. Augustine	St. Jane Frances de Chantal	St. Pio of Pietrelcina (Padre Pio)
St. Benedict	St. Joan of Arc	St. Rita of Cascia
St. Blaise	St. John Bosco	St. Rose of Lima
St. Boniface	St. John Henry Newman	St. Teresa Benedicta of the Cross
St. Catherine of Siena	St. John Vianney	St. Teresa of Avila
St. Cecilia	St. Jude	St. Teresa of Calcutta
St. Clare of Assisi	St. Katharine Drexel	St. Thomas More
St. Clement	St. Maria Goretti	St. Vincent de Paul
	St. Mary MacKillop	

A LIST OF WORDS TO INSPIRE

adapt	focus	jump	release	trust
courage	grow	love	rest	wonder
enjoy	heal	new	shift	yes
enough	hope	pause	strive	

EPIPHANY (THREE KINGS)

Epiphany is a word that comes from a Greek term for "manifestation" and refers to the three magi—also known as wise men or kings—visiting Jesus after his birth. Around the world, Three Kings Day is celebrated even more widely than Christmas and is traditionally the day when families exchange gifts, symbolizing the gifts that the wise men brought to Jesus.

Pope Francis said in his 2019 address that, like the three kings, "we need to *arise*, to get up from our sedentary lives and prepare for a journey."[1] Meditate on how God might be calling you to a new journey.

Enjoy Rosca de Reyes *(Three Kings Bread)*

Either buy or make the *rosca de reyes* (three kings bread). This sweet bread comes from the Mexican tradition and contains a baby Jesus doll hidden inside. It is said that whoever ends up with the baby Jesus doll in their slice of cake on Three Kings Day is obligated to host a party for Candlemas, which occurs on February 2.

Enjoy Mexican-style hot chocolate along with it.

Make Kings' Crowns

* Gold poster board, cut into crown shapes
* Craft glue
* Plastic gems, glass beads, or small charms for decorating
* Glitter (if you dare)
* Stapler

Offer each child a pre-cut crown from gold poster board. Let everyone get creative with lots of fun and sparkly supplies to decorate their own crown. After decorating, staple the crown's ends together so that it can be worn.

Make a Gold, Frankincense, and Myrrh Diffuser

The three kings brought gifts of gold, frankincense, and myrrh: gold signified that Jesus is the King of kings, frankincense was used for worship and prayer, and myrrh was used for embalming a corpse and foretold Jesus's death.

* Shallow ceramic or glass bowl
* Gold leaf sheets
* Metal leaf adhesive
* Paintbrush
* 1 cup pink Himalayan salt
* Frankincense and myrrh essential oils
* Votive candle

Follow the instructions on the gold leaf sheets and metal leaf adhesive to adhere gold and metal around the outside of the bowl using the paintbrush. In another bowl, mix the salt with your essential oils; you will need about 20 drops total per cup of salt. Then pour the salt into your bowl and push your votive candle in the middle. When the salt is warmed by the flame, it will diffuse the smell of the frankincense and myrrh into the air. Keep the diffuser near where you sit to pray.

Bless Your Home with Chalk

Ask your local church if there is blessed chalk to take home. Gather some holy water from your parish as well.

Using the blessed chalk, mark the lintel of your front door (or front porch step) with the initials of the three wise men, connected with crosses. Then write the year, breaking up the numbers and the year so that they fall on both sides of the initials as follows:

20 + C + M + B + 23

The C stands for Caspar, M for Melchoir, and B for Balthasar. These initials also stand for *Christus mansionem benedicat*, which means, "Christ, bless this house."

Then say aloud the following prayers:

The three wise men—Caspar, Melchior, and Balthazar—followed the star of
God's Son who became human two thousand and _____ years ago.
May Christ bless our home and remain with us throughout the new year. Amen.

Visit, O blessed Lord, this home with the gladness of your presence. Bless all who live or visit here with the gift of your love; and grant that we may manifest your love to each other and to all whose lives we touch. May we grow in grace and in the knowledge and love of you; guide, comfort, and strengthen us in peace, O Jesus Christ, now and forever. Amen.

After the prayers of the blessing are recited, walk through the house. Sprinkle holy water into each room while praying, "Bless this room and bring its inhabitants your peace."

20 + C + M + B + 23

BAPTISM OF OUR LORD

The Sunday after Epiphany, we honor Jesus's baptism and the beginning of his public ministry at age thirty. When John the Baptist baptized Jesus, the Holy Spirit came down in the form of a dove, and God the Father announced Jesus's place as his Son. With this, Jesus was sent out to proclaim the Gospel. This feast also highlights the humility of Jesus, who submitted himself to John even when John said Jesus was his superior. We celebrate Jesus's desire to become one with us in all things except sin, and we ask the Holy Spirit to guide us to minister to his people.

Style a Scalloped Shell Purse with Your Outfit

The scalloped shell has been used in many baptisms because it was widely available near water and was a good vessel for scooping and pouring water. Grab a shell purse for church as a mini symbol of the Christian pilgrimage of baptism.

Add Your Baptism Date to Your Calendar

If you don't know the date of your own baptism, ask your parents or call the church where you were baptized. Add this date to your calendar to celebrate and thank God on that date.

Use Scalloped Shells

Hang a scalloped shell in your home or prayer space, use shells in a sensory bin, or make little scalloped shell felt crafts.

Stay Hydrated

Water is both cleansing and purifying. Drink enough water today and make it a goal to do so for the entire month. Each time you take a sip, say the prayer, "Jesus, I trust in you" or "Come, Holy Spirit."

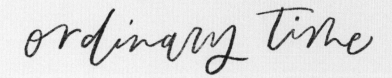

ordinary time

CELEBRATING THE MYSTERY OF JESUS'S LIFE

ORDINARY TIME I,
THE DAY AFTER THE BAPTISM OF
OUR LORD UP TO ASH WEDNESDAY

ORDINARY TIME I

*We are frequently tempted to think that holiness is only for those who
can withdraw from ordinary affairs to spend much time in prayer. That is
not the case.... We are all called to be holy by living our lives with love
and by bearing witness to everything we do, wherever we find ourselves.*
—Pope Francis, Gaudete et Exultate (Rejoice and Be Glad)

Ordinary Time is one season split into two periods of the year, and it chronicles Jesus's ministry. We often think of it as the time in between the more notable seasons like Advent and Christmas, Lent and Easter. But it serves an important purpose in our spiritual lives. Although birthdays and celebrations are fun and exciting, it is mostly the ordinary days we spend in our homes that make up our lives.

This concept reminds me of how I often show up in my therapist's office with some crisis. I have an objective as I walk into the room. It is usually a problem to solve or a situation to explore. But on occasion, nothing major has happened and I show up without an agenda. Sometimes I even think I shouldn't go, but I show up anyway. And it is in those sessions that I usually have the biggest revelations. Without any expectations or crises to tend to, more can be revealed.

Ordinary Time is similar. It is a season for growth, a season for tending to the garden and allowing what will be to be. In celebrating feast days during this time, we are reminded to see God not just in the big moments of our lives but also in simple rhythms. God isn't only present in special occasions, but he is also with us in our morning coffee routines, in our workplaces, and in our household chores.

We can train ourselves to always have our hearts inclined to see him.

We are all called
to be holy by living
our lives with love...

Protect us, Lord,
as we stay awake;
watch over us
as we sleep,
that awake,
we may keep
watch with Christ,
and asleep,
rest in his peace.

PRESENTATION OF OUR LORD (CANDLEMAS)

FEBRUARY 2

It was Jewish custom to present infants in the Temple in order to dedicate the child to God and to pray over the new mother. When Mary and Joseph dutifully brought Jesus to the Temple, they were fulfilling their promises to God and stepping into their roles as the earthly parents of Jesus.

Make Beeswax Candles

With this activity, contemplate the mystery of Christ being fully human and fully divine. Beeswax is extracted by virgin bees (worker bees who do not take part in the reproductive process in the hive) and symbolizes the pure flesh of Jesus born of the Virgin Mary. As you make a candle, think about Christ's purity as he took flesh and became fully human without sin. St. Anselm wrote that the wick of the candle is a symbol of the soul of Christ and that the flame is a symbol of Christ's divinity.[1] As you light the candles, meditate on his divine nature.

* Beeswax candle-making kit
* Modeling beeswax (optional)
* Hair dryer
* Knife or scissors

There are some easy kits for rolling or pouring beeswax candles that you can purchase to make your own candles. We added some color to ours by decorating with modeling beeswax, too; one tip is to warm the wax with a hair dryer to make it more malleable.

Take these candles to Mass for a traditional blessing.

Enjoy Pancakes

It's traditional to eat pancakes (or crepes in France) on Candlemas. The golden discs of pancakes are a reminder of the sun, which represents the Son of God, the true Light of the world. An old saying goes that if you eat pancakes on Candlemas, you will be assured a good harvest in the coming year.

Make pancakes for breakfast today to celebrate the Presentation.

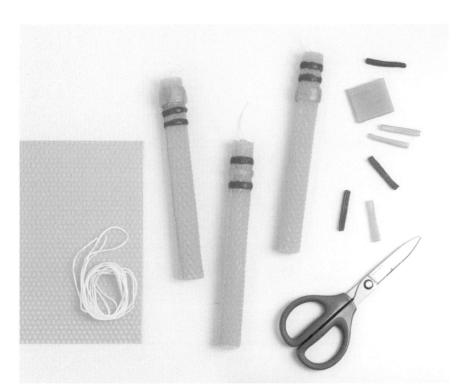

Eat Tamales

In Mexico, it's traditional to celebrate with tamales. Have a tamale dinner party today! (Don't forget: whoever had the baby Jesus in their slice of *rosca de reyes* (p. 52) on Epiphany has to host the party today!)

Night Prayer

When Mary and Joseph went to present Jesus in the Temple, they encountered the prophet Simeon, who immediately recognized the infant Jesus as the Messiah and spoke words recorded in Luke's gospel and recited in the Church's prayer every night.

Praying Simeon's canticle is a beautiful way to end the day. It can be sung or read easily in just a few minutes before bed. In many communities, this is when forgiveness is asked of others and gratitude is given for kindnesses throughout the day. This is a beautiful tradition to incorporate into your spiritual life.

Lord, now you let your servant go in peace; your word has been fulfilled: my own eyes have seen the salvation that you have prepared in the sight of every people: a light to reveal you to the nations and the glory of your people Israel.

Glory to the Father, and to the Son, and to the Holy Spirit: as it was in the beginning, is now, and will be forever. Amen.

RESPONSE: *Protect us, Lord, as we stay awake; watch over us as we sleep, that awake, we may keep watch with Christ, and asleep, rest in his peace.*

ST. JOSEPHINE BAKHITA

FEBRUARY 8

Born circa 1869 in Olgossa, Sultanate of Darfur
(present-day Sudan)
Died 1947 in Schio, Italy

PATRON SAINT OF: Sudan, human-trafficking survivors

The first Black woman declared a saint in the modern era, St. Josephine Bakhita was born in Sudan, kidnapped and sold into slavery at age seven, and eventually taken to Italy. It was in Italy that she discovered the Catholic faith, fought for her freedom by winning a legal battle, and became a religious sister.

Stargaze

> *Seeing the sun, the moon, and the stars, I said to myself,*
> *who could be the Master of these beautiful things?*
> *And I felt a great desire to see him, to know him, and to pay him homage.*
> *—St. Josephine Bakhita*

If it's a clear night, bundle up and go outside to gaze at the stars. Contemplate the vastness of God. If you can't see stars well from your neighborhood, it could be fun to pack the car and drive out to a more remote area with less light pollution. Without city and street lights, the night sky will come alive.

Donate to an Organization
That Aids Victims of Human Trafficking

St. Josephine Bakhita is the patron saint of victims of human trafficking. Research the horrors of human trafficking that exist today and make a donation to an organization that helps those who have been trafficked.

Find Freedom in Your Life

Find a cozy spot to sit in prayer. Invite God to enlighten you to the areas of your life in which you are not free. What enslaves you? Your phone? An addiction? Resentment? A relationship? Be totally honest with yourself and ask God to free you.

Journal about ways that you can find freedom and research resources to help you. Ask St. Josephine to pray for you.

OUR LADY OF LOURDES

FEBRUARY 11

Our Lady of Lourdes is a Marian apparition that took place in Lourdes, France. She appeared eighteen times to illiterate, impoverished fourteen-year-old St. Bernadette in 1858. The waters at Lourdes are known to have miraculous healing capabilities.

Bless Your Life with Healing Water

The waters of Lourdes have brought healing to hundreds of people. Even though you might not be able to visit, you can still bless your life with the healing water that God created and is all around us.

* Be mindful to drink the recommended eight to eleven glasses of water today.
* Bless yourself with holy water before you leave the house for the day. If you have kids, let them do this, too. You can even get a home holy water font to keep year-round.
* Take a refreshing bath.
* Water your garden (and the plants in your house that you may have neglected).

Create a Tiny Grotto

Mary appeared to Bernadette Soubirous at a grotto in France. From the darkness came a light, and a figure appeared who was dressed in white, with a blue belt at her waist, two golden-yellow roses on her feet, and a yellow rosary in her hands.

* Polymer oven bake clay
* 3-inch statue or a printed photo of Mary
* Scissors
* Acrylic paint
* Paintbrushes
* Glue
* Tiny dried plants

Roll your clay into a small ball and punch your thumb into the middle. Mold the clay into an arched form like a tiny grotto. Bake according to the package. Meanwhile, paint the Mary statue or cut out a tiny picture of Our Lady of Lourdes. Once the grotto has cured and cooled, glue Mary into the middle. You can decorate the outside with small dried leaves or flowers.

Little ones delight in having a tiny Mary for their bedrooms. Consider making one for your desk at work.

SHROVE TUESDAY

The Tuesday before Lent has many names and is celebrated in different ways around the world. The first word in "Shrove Tuesday," for example, means "to confess," as it was customary to go to Confession before the beginning of Lent. Historically there is a widespread custom of using all the fats, meats, and dairy products in the house before entering into the Lenten season of fasting and abstinence. This led to nicknames in Louisiana and France of "Mardi Gras" (Fat Tuesday), and in Latin American countries it is known as "Carnival" (Farewell to Meat). It is a day of great indulgence in rich foods and celebration before entering into the penitential season of Lent.

Enjoy a King Cake

Like they do in New Orleans, eat a king cake. You can even decorate an angel food cake in purple and green if you can't find a real king cake. Similar to the *rosca de reyes* (p. 52), a king cake can contain a baby Jesus for someone to find and be crowned king!

Eat Your Favorite Foods

Indulge in your favorite foods as a last hoorah before the fasting and prayer of the Lenten season. I like to go to In-N-Out Burger for burgers and fries.

Have a Picnic

In Greece, it's custom to celebrate "Clean Monday" on the Monday before Ash Wednesday by going for a picnic and flying kites.

Have Fun with a Piñata

The Sunday before Lent in Denmark, people fill a piñata-like barrel with candy. Whoever breaks the piñata is crowned the Cat King or Cat Queen (because the barrel used to contain a live cat instead of candy).

You can print out our cat masks using the "Cat Masks" template. Use string or ribbon to tie them over your face. Use blankets for capes or buy king and queen dress-up sets for the winners to wear. We also made felt crowns, but you could also use the crowns from Epiphany (p. 52).

Make Masks or Headdresses

Use sparkly things, feathers, and gems to decorate store-bought masks like in New Orleans or headdresses like in Brazil.

Go to Confession

Prepare yourself for Lent with a clean soul.

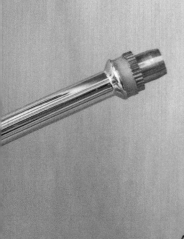

lent

A TIME OF FASTING, PRAYER,
AND PENANCE IN PREPARATION
FOR CHRIST'S RESURRECTION

ASH WEDNESDAY THROUGH
THE EVENING CELEBRATION
OF HOLY THURSDAY

LENT

We plant seeds that will flower as results in our lives,
so best to remove the weeds of anger, avarice, envy
and doubt, that peace and abundance may manifest for all.
—Dorothy Day

My spiritual director once told me to enter the desert for Lent. I grew up in the Sonoran Desert of Arizona, and while that is different from the desert of the Holy Land, I think it has Lenten lessons to teach us. Many people think that the desert is just hot, dry, and brown without much life. However, even in the scorching sun, the desert blooms, too. Often in times of spiritual dryness, we think that nothing can come of it, nothing can come of us. We feel abandoned or left out to shrivel. But if God made gorgeous red flowers blossom out of cacti, can't we believe that God can make something sprout from our desert, too?

As we move through the season of Lent, we can ask God to help us see the bustling life around us. We take only the necessities into the desert—lots of water, sunscreen, and a sun hat. And we ask God to open our eyes to see the gecko scurrying in the shade, to open our ears to hear the chirping of the cactus wren, to quiet the chatter of our minds to feel the warmth of the sun. In this practice, we can begin to see God in the kindness of a stranger holding the door for us at the grocery store, in the migrant family who needs clothing for their children, in the dishes that need to be washed once again. Lenten practices do not need to be like our overzealous New Year's resolutions that are abandoned within a few weeks. The Church gives us three simple pillars to focus on during this time that are not meant just as punishment or trials of our self-will (to give up chocolate). These three pillars are prayer, fasting, and almsgiving. As we journey into the desert with Jesus, our focus shifts to decluttering our lives to create room for God. And in what can feel like desolation and loneliness, may we know that God's love blossoms there, too. There is often more beauty and growth in the "beginning again" than in doing it perfectly.

peace and abundance
may manifest for all

AT THE BEGINNING OF LENT

Make Cardboard Cacti

Create a space in your home that reminds you of this season by decorating with cacti. Of course they naturally exist in a different kind of desert, but they will be a visual reminder of the spiritual desert. Set them up in a prayer corner, or even put one in every room so that you have touch points in all of your spaces, like by your toothbrush. Then, whenever you see one—like when you're brushing your teeth—you will be reminded of your Lenten practices.

If you're in a climate that isn't cactus friendly or if you have small pets or children, you could make this DIY version instead.

* Cardboard
* Pencil
* Scissors or box cutter
* Acrylic paint in green and white
* Paintbrush
* Terra-cotta pots (or cups to paint)
* Soil or craft paper

For each cactus, draw a cactus shape on cardboard. Cut 2 copies. Lay them next to each other and with a scissors or box cutter make a small slit up from the bottom on one and down from the top on the other. Slide them into each other to test that they sit well together, then take apart and paint green. You can paint little spikes with white as well. Once dry, put them together and "plant" them in pots filled with soil or craft paper. Place in your prayer corner as a reminder of the Lenten desert.

THROUGHOUT THE SEASON OF LENT

Practice the Three Pillars of Lent

Choose from these simple ideas to practice the three pillars of Lent.

Praying

* Write down one thing you're grateful for every day.
* Pray one Hail Mary before bed.
* Listen to one soothing playlist on repeat all Lent.
* Set a timer to sit in silence for one minute each day.
* Read the four gospels and Acts.

Fasting (Giving Up)

* Avoid beating yourself up if your day didn't go as planned.
* Avoid watching TV with dark or overly intense imagery.
* Avoid listening to music, podcasts, or audiobooks in the car (allowing for more silence).
* Avoid cussing.
* Avoid avoiding your emotions.
* Avoid nonessential spending.

Instead, try the following:

* Drink more water and eating more vegetables.
* Read a book before bed (instead of phone scrolling).
* Take a walk every day.

Almsgiving

* Every week, send a heartfelt affirmation text to a friend or family member (bonus if it's a handwritten card).
* Donate five dollars per week to an organization that serves the poor.
* Make "Blessings Bags" (p. 198) and keep them in your car to hand out to the poor you encounter.
* Volunteer at a soup kitchen or a food pantry.

I find using a tracker helps me practice the three pillars; download and print the "Lenten Practices Tracker" from our templates if you want to use one, too.

FRIDAYS IN LENT

Go Meatless

We give up meat on Fridays in Lent as an act of penance and sacrifice, to remind us of the ultimate sacrifice of Jesus Christ on the cross, and to focus on our spiritual journey and repentance during this holy season.

Pray the Stations of the Cross

Another Lenten tradition on Fridays is to pray the Stations of the Cross in remembrance of Christ's sacrifice for us. You can either do this at home or find a local church that is participating in this practice on Fridays.

On the Fourth Friday of Lent

Make Fruit Popsicles for La Samaritana

In Mexico, the fourth Friday of Lent is a special celebration called "La Samaritana." On this day, people hand out water, fruit, and ice cream in honor of the Samaritan woman whom Jesus met at the well and who gave him water. You could make popsicles with fresh fruit or just buy some from the store.

SUNDAYS IN LENT

Fasting is set aside and prayers are said standing,
as a sign of the Resurrection . . . on every Sunday.
—St. Augustine

Since its beginning, the Church has viewed Sunday as a day of celebration and remembrance of the Resurrection. Sunday is considered a "little Easter." Sundays in Lent do indeed count as days in the Lenten season, but it's important that the character of joy on Sundays is not completely done away with. It is everyone's personal decision regarding their fasting practices on Sundays. But remember that feasting on Sundays in remembrance of the Resurrection is always encouraged in some way!

Celebrate the Resurrection on Sundays in Lent

Choose from these ideas to celebrate the Resurrection on Lenten Sundays:

* Enjoy a small dessert.
* Rest from your Lenten fasting practice.
* Read from the Acts of the Apostles.
* Make a fancier dinner than normal or order takeout.

Celebrate Mothering Sunday

Most Sundays people go to their nearest parish or "daughter church." Traditionally in England, in the middle of Lent, everyone would visit their "mother church" where they were baptized. The fourth Sunday of Lent became known as Mothering Sunday because people would also visit their mothers. On this fourth Sunday, visit the church where you were baptized if you can, or look at pictures from your baptism. Bring flowers to your mom or call her.

STS. PERPETUA AND FELICITY

MARCH 7

Born circa 182 near Carthage, North Africa
Died circa 203 in Carthage, Roman Province of Africa

PATRON SAINTS OF: Mothers, expectant mothers, ranchers, butchers, Carthage, Catalonia

Sts. Perpetua and Felicity were martyrs who refused to renounce their Christian faith. Felicity was an enslaved woman and expectant mother (who gave birth in prison just days before her martyrdom). Perpetua was a twenty-two-year-old noblewoman who was nursing a baby boy. They were both imprisoned together and were killed together in a Roman arena.

Make Friendship Bracelets

Perpetua and Felicity were best friends. Make friendship bracelets with a friend or by yourself and give to a friend with a note describing what you love about them. All you need is some embroidery thread, and there are lots of different patterns for different skill levels online.

Sing Your Favorite Song

How often do you allow yourself to sing? Perpetua led the group of martyrs into the Roman arena singing while looking joyful and calm. Sing your favorite song out loud. You could even play a fun game of karaoke.

Write about Your Faith

Perpetua's diary of her martyrdom is the earliest firsthand account of martyrdom written by a woman. She wrote about her deep faith in God, and it continues to inspire future generations.

Write in a physical journal or online about your faith journey. Share it publicly, if it feels right, or save it for future generations to find.

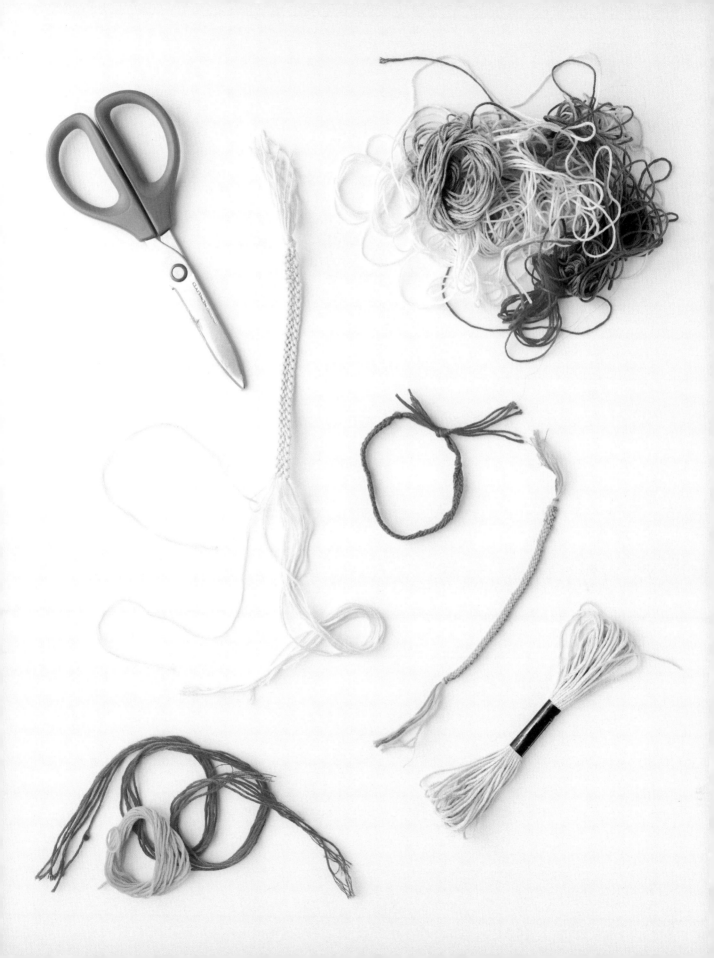

ST. PATRICK

MARCH 17

Born circa 385 in Roman Britain
(present-day Great Britain)
Died circa 461 in Gaelic Ireland
(present-day Northern Ireland)

PATRON SAINT OF: Ireland, engineers

Even though St. Patrick suffered greatly while enslaved for six years at the hands of the Irish druids, he willingly returned to Ireland a few years after escaping because he had a vision and felt that God was calling him to love the Irish people and tell them about Jesus.

Wear Green or Eat Green or Irish-Inspired Food

* Avocado toast
* Green smoothie
* Charred broccoli
* Irish soda bread
* Shepherd's pie

Fast from Alcohol as the Early Catholics in Ireland

Early Catholics actually *fasted* from alcohol on St. Patrick's Day, which is different from how it has come to be celebrated today. Maybe drink S.Pellegrino or Lime LaCroix instead because they have green containers.

Make a Shamrock

St. Patrick used the shamrock to meditate on the Holy Trinity.

* "Shamrock" template
* Air-dry clay
* Metal loop or jump ring
* Rolling pin
* Clay tools
* Acrylic paint
* Paintbrush

Roll out some air-dry clay and use the template to cut out a shamrock shape. Smooth the edges and stick a metal loop or jump ring through the top for hanging. Let it dry according to the package instructions, then paint it green. Hang the shamrock in your home year-round for a daily reminder of the Trinity.

You could alternatively make shamrock-shaped cookies!

Combat Self-Doubt

Write in your journal (as St. Patrick did often in his *Confessio*) and reflect honestly on your day.

* What are three ways I succeeded today?
* What are three things I could have done better?

Cultivate Gratitude

St. Patrick wrote, "I will not be silent because of my desire for thanksgiving." Though he believed himself to be imperfect, he continued to minister and serve anyway. Most of his energy to serve came through his practice of gratitude for God's blessings. You can make a gratitude journal like on page 169.

Frame St. Patrick's Breastplate

Practice your penmanship by writing "St. Patrick's Breastplate," then hang it in your home (maybe next to your shamrock). You can also print out my hand-lettered, downloadable version to hang up.

Christ with me,
Christ before me,
Christ behind me,
Christ in me,
Christ beneath me,
Christ above me,
Christ on my right,
Christ on my left,
Christ when I lie down,
Christ when I sit down,
Christ when I arise,
Christ in the heart of every man who thinks of me,
Christ in the mouth of everyone who speaks of me,
Christ in every eye that sees me,
Christ in every ear that hears me.

Christ be with me,
Christ within me,
Christ behind me,
Christ before me,
Christ beside me,
Christ to win me,
Christ to comfort and
restore me,
Christ beneath me,
Christ above me,
Christ in quiet,
Christ in danger,
Christ in hearts
of all who
love me.

THE BREASTPLATE OF ST. PATRICK

ST. JOSEPH

MARCH 19

PATRON SAINT OF: Universal Catholic Church, families, fathers, expectant mothers, travelers, immigrants, house sellers and buyers, craftsmen, engineers, working people, married people, persons living in exile, the sick and dying, a holy death

St. Joseph was the husband of Mary and Jesus's foster father.

Write a Letter to a Father

Write a letter to your own father, a spiritual father, or a new father. Tell them all the things that you love about them.

Help Children in Foster Care

Joseph was the foster father of Jesus. Reach out to the foster system in your area and ask what their needs are. Often they are in need of suitcases or backpacks so that children can carry their belongings. Donate new or gently used items that you collect from your home or community.

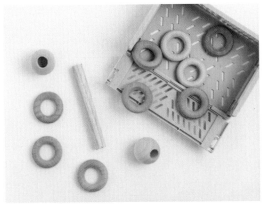

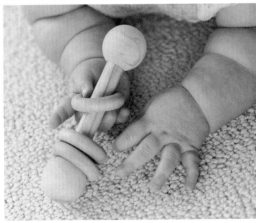

Make a Wooden Baby Rattle

Joseph was a carpenter, and we can imagine that he made wooden toys for his son. Make these simple rattles as baby gifts for someone you know, or donate to a pregnancy center.

* ½-inch wooden dowel, cut to 3 inches
* 2 rounded dowel caps, 1¼ inches with ½-inch hole
* 3 wooden rings, 1½-inch diameter
* Nontoxic wood glue

If necessary, sand the wood parts smooth. Glue one end of the dowel into a dowel cap with wood glue. Slide the three rings over the other end, and then glue on the second dowel cap. Let the glue dry.

Spend Time in Silence

Pope Francis wrote that in St. Joseph "we never see frustration, but only trust. His patient silence was the prelude to concrete expressions of trust."[1]

Spend fifteen minutes in silence today and reflect on where you can be more trusting of God's ways in your life.

ST. ÓSCAR ROMERO

MARCH 24

Born 1917 in Ciudad Barrios, El Salvador
Died 1980 in San Salvador, El Salvador

PATRON SAINT OF: Christian communicators, El Salvador, the Americas, persecuted Christians, Archdiocese of San Salvador

St. Óscar Romero became Archbishop of San Salvador, El Salvador, in 1977, at a time of widespread violence and great unrest in his country. He was known to be timid and considered a "safe" choice as archbishop so as not to cause trouble. Against all expectations, he began publicly speaking out against the injustice happening in El Salvador in the last three years of his life. He was most known for his radio homilies that gave hope to the people of El Salvador during this turbulent time. He was assassinated while celebrating Mass in 1980.

Eat Pupusas and Tamales

Make or buy pupusas or tamales, which are food specialties from El Salvador.

Fight for Injustice

Óscar Romero was spurred to action when his friend was murdered while fighting against injustice in El Salvador. What injustices do you see in the world that you feel called to speak out about? Write a letter to your local leaders advocating for the rights of the poor. Join an advocacy network. Make a plan to take action.

Make an El Salvadoran Folk Art Cross

* "El Salvadoran Folk Art Cross" template
* Wooden cross or cardboard cut into a cross shape
* Pencil
* Acrylic paint
* Paintbrush

The Romero cross was designed in honor of St. Óscar Romero in traditional El Salvadoran folk-art style. The images represent the life of Jesus, the Trinity, and the people of El Salvador. Draw and paint your own cross, using the template to trace the symbols you want to use.

ANNUNCIATION

MARCH 25

On the Annunciation of the Lord, we celebrate when the angel Gabriel visited Mary to announce that she would bear the Son of God and Mary's yes to that call. Venerable Fulton J. Sheen said, "In the garden of her womb, Mary would bring Redemption."[2] Today, we are relieved of our Lenten fast and can eat meat!

Pray a Nature Rosary

Take a group nature walk in silence. Each person collects small objects in a basket—rocks, leaves, mushrooms, pods, nuts, sticks, and so on. The leader should collect six rocks, two sticks, and three found objects, and then set out a string (twine, yarn, or a rope) in the shape of a rosary. Bring everyone back together to begin the prayer. Assign someone to be in charge of each decade or prayer.

To pray the nature Rosary, lay a found object out for each "bead" of the rosary, as follows. The leader begins by arranging two sticks in the shape of a cross at the end of the string and reciting the Apostles' Creed. Then they place one rock above it and pray the Our Father. Next, they pray three Hail Marys as they place each of the three found objects—for faith, hope, and charity. With the next rock, they pray the Glory Be and the O My Jesus prayers.

Then the first decade is announced. The person in charge of that decade will pray the Our Father. Then, as they lay out ten found objects, they pray ten Hail Marys, followed by a Glory Be and O My Jesus. The leader places a rock for each Our Father bead. Repeat for all five decades, allowing each person to lead the decade to which they are assigned. When everyone is finished, the leader ends the Rosary with a Hail, Holy Queen prayer.

Create a Giftable Mary Garden

* "Giftable Mary Garden" template
* Seed paper
* Flower-shaped paper punch
* Watercolor paints
* Paintbrush
* Cellophane bags, each 4 x 6 inches
* Cardstock
* Stapler
* Printer
* Scissors

Print and cut the template on cardstock. Paint the seed paper with watercolors and let it dry. Punch out lots of flowers from the seed paper with the paper punch to make seed-paper confetti. Fill the cellophane baggies with the flowers and staple the template-printed cardstock on top of each. Hand out to friends to "plant" and make their own Mary Gardens.

Make a Fiat Wall Decor

* Paper
* Marker or pen
* Tape
* Armature wire
* Needle-nose pliers (optional but useful)
* Wire snips
* Embroidery thread (optional)

The yes that Mary gave is called her *fiat*. Write out the word *fiat* in cursive on a big piece of paper. Tape the paper to a flat, sturdy surface, such as a table. Use needle-nose pliers to shape the armature wire to match the cursive, taping down the wire as you work for stability. Once you've reached the end, cut the wire to size. Leave as is or wrap with embroidery thread before hanging on a wall.

Make Edible Flower Lollipops

* 2 cups sugar
* ⅔ cup water
* ⅛ teaspoon cream of tartar
* Spoon or whisk
* 2–3 drops flavoring oil
* Measuring cup
* Edible dried flowers
* Small pot
* Kitchen thermometer
* Lollipop molds and sticks

Make these lollipops to recall the "garden of Mary's womb." Combine the sugar, cream of tartar, and water in a pot. Stir them together until it is dissolved. Boil the mixture until it's 290°F. Remove the pot from the heat, and when it stops bubbling, add the flavoring oil.

Using a measuring cup for ease of pouring, pour a little bit into the mold for each lollipop. Sprinkle on a few dried flowers and then cover with more of the mixture. Insert the lollipop sticks. Let cool and harden before gifting or enjoying!

Eat Waffles or Seed Cake

The word for "waffle" in Swedish is very close to the term for "Virgin Mary," so it became the traditional Annunciation food. Enjoy a waffle today, adding strawberries to symbolize Mary's fruitfulness (see p. 10).

England's traditional Annunciation food is the seed cake, which symbolizes Jesus, who became flesh as a seed in Mary's womb. Enjoy a seed cake in memory of Mary's motherhood.

Buy Some Madonna Lilies

The *Lilium candidum*, or Madonna lily, is a symbol of the Annunciation. You can see it in paintings of the archangel Gabriel bringing the message to Mary as well as in paintings of Joseph, who was to care for Mary and the Son of God. Purchase some Madonna lilies for your home to celebrate the Annunciation.

holy week

A WEEK TO REMEMBER
CHRIST'S SUFFERING, DEATH,
AND RESURRECTION

PALM SUNDAY THROUGH
HOLY SATURDAY

PALM SUNDAY

Palm Sunday is the Sunday before Holy Week begins. We remember and celebrate Jesus's entrance into Jerusalem by holding palm leaves and singing "Hosanna" as we also solemnly prepare our hearts for Jesus's Passion and death.

Wear Red

Red is the color of fire and symbolizes the presence of God's Holy Spirit and the sacrifices of martyrs. Pentecost is the only Sunday for red in the liturgical calendar.

Decorate with Pussy Willows or Palms

In Latvia and Bulgaria, pussy willows are easier to find than palms, so they use them instead of palms and call Palm Sunday Pussy Willow Sunday. You can decorate with pussy willows or dried palms.

Make Palm Frond Rings

Ethiopians call Palm Sunday "Hosanna," and they weave palm fronds into elaborate rings to wear. Look up a video tutorial on making palm frond rings and try making your own.

Take a Walk

Imagine Jesus entering your neighborhood triumphantly and herald him in your heart.

HOLY MONDAY

On Holy Monday we remember Jesus visiting his friends at Bethany and Mary anointing him with precious oil, preparing him for his burial. Many dioceses hold their Chrism Mass on Holy Monday, during which the priests of the diocese gather as the bishop consecrates and distributes to each parish the sacred oils used in the Sacraments of Baptism, Confirmation, and Holy Orders.

Pray Psalm 21

Pray with Psalm 21 this week. In it we see through the eyes of David the picture of Christ suffering for us on the Cross.

Bless Yourself and Your Family with Oil

Ask your priest to bless olive oil for you to use in your home. On Holy Monday, bless yourself and each member of your household with the blessed oil and a Sign of the Cross. It can serve as a simple reminder of penitence as we enter into Holy Week.

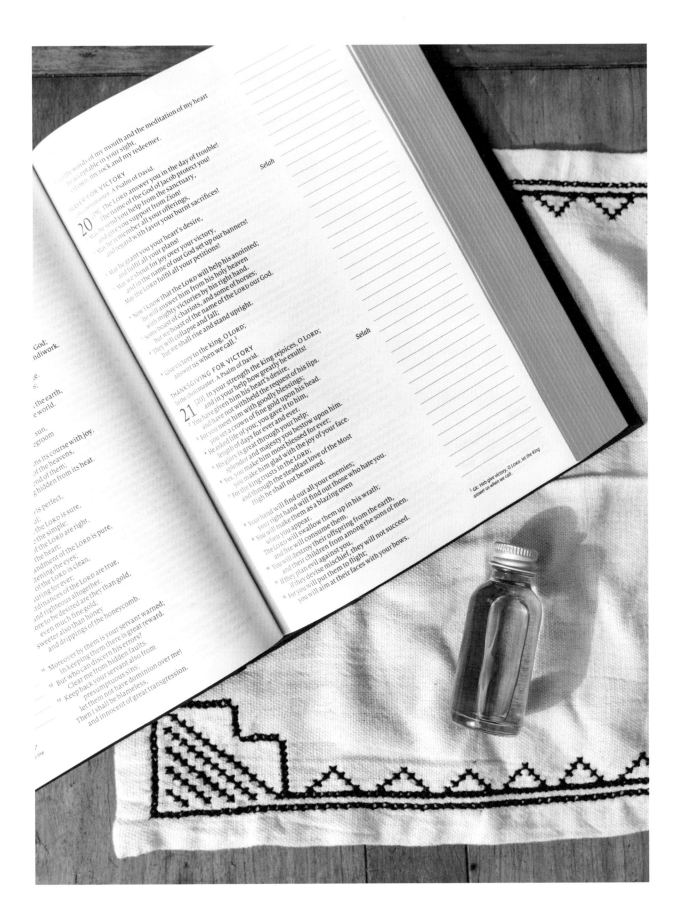

HOLY TUESDAY

On Holy Tuesday, we remember Jesus's announcement of Judas's and Peter's denial.

Perform a Secret Service

If you are in a household group, create slips of paper with a need each person has and place them in a container. (If you are digitally connected, use an online name-drawer website to create the same experience.) Each person then draws a need from the bin and anonymously tries to help or support the need by giving service during the upcoming Easter season. This is a simple yet intentional way to follow the commandment to love one another.

Clean Your House

Spring housecleaning is an ancient tradition, going back to the customs of the Jewish families preparing for the Passover. When we clean our homes during Holy Week, we prepare the house for the glory of the Resurrection.

HOLY WEDNESDAY (SPY WEDNESDAY)

The day before Judas betrays Jesus, he visits the chief priests and is promised thirty pieces of silver in exchange for delivering Jesus to them. Spy Wednesday gets its name in reference to the "spy" or "traitor" Judas.

Donate to a Charity

Holy Wednesday is also known as Spy Wednesday because Judas betrayed Jesus for thirty coins. Give thirty quarters ($7.50) to a charity that has meaning for you.

Reflect in Silence

None of us is free from sin, and it hurts to look at. Spy Wednesday is an opportunity to reflect on the ways we have been like Judas to Jesus, the ways we have failed our friends or even betrayed those we love the most. Reflect in silence today about ways you have betrayed Jesus in your own heart and seek forgiveness.

HOLY THURSDAY (MAUNDY THURSDAY)

The Last Supper is celebrated today as we remember Jesus making his final preparations for his Passion. The Eucharist and Sacrament of Holy Orders are both instituted on this day in our tradition. *Maundy* comes from the word *maundatum*, which refers to Jesus's commandment to "love one another." This commandment of love is symbolized by the washing of the feet of the apostles, often reenacted at Mass. Typically after Mass, the Eucharist is processed throughout the church and then placed on a separate "altar of repose" for adoration until midnight in memory of Jesus's agony in the Garden of Gethsemane. If you're unable to attend Mass on Holy Thursday, consider having your own foot-washing ceremony at home. You could read Mark 10:43-45 together and discuss what service looks like in your family.

Make Unleavened Bread

* 1 cup flour, plus extra for countertop
* ⅓ cup Perrier or other sparkling water
* 1 tablespoon light olive oil
* 1–2 tablespoon honey
* Parchment paper
* Baking sheet

Preheat the oven to 425°F. Mix all ingredients thoroughly. Turn onto a lightly floured countertop and knead into a ball. Divide into 6 portions and shape each into a ball. Flatten each into a 3-inch round. Bake on a parchment-paper-lined baking sheet for 8–10 minutes.

Donate Socks or Shoes

Many homeless shelters offer foot care because those who live on the streets are on their feet all day long. Call a local shelter and see what they need. Consider donating socks or shoes to the shelter.

Write a Letter to a Priest

Since Holy Thursday is when we celebrate the institution of the priesthood, it's a great time to write a letter to a priest who changed your life. Pray a special prayer for him.

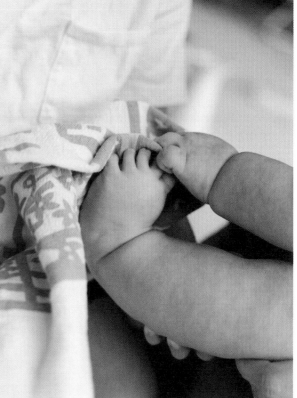

GOOD FRIDAY

Good Friday is the most somber day of the year for Christians. Contrary to every other day of the year, Mass is not celebrated anywhere in the world on this day. A commemoration of Christ's Passion is typically held between 12 p.m. and 3 p.m. with a liturgy that includes a recitation of the Passion and Veneration of the Cross.

Today we abstain from meat and fast from regular meals, which helps us to be more mindful of those who suffer in so many ways. We join our sufferings and worries to those of Christ crucified and trust in him.

Create Your Own Stations of the Cross

The Stations of the Cross is a meditative prayer that commemorates the events of Jesus's last day on earth. A series of fourteen pictures or carvings portray the suffering, Passion, and death of Jesus.

Find fourteen images from current news where there is suffering in the world and pair them with each of the fourteen stations:

I. Jesus is condemned to death.

II. Jesus carries his Cross.

III. Jesus falls the first time.

IV. Jesus meets his mother.

V. Simon of Cyrene helps Jesus to carry his Cross.

VI. Veronica wipes the face of Jesus.

VII. Jesus falls the second time.

VIII. Jesus meets the women of Jerusalem.

IX. Jesus falls a third time.

X. Jesus's clothes are taken away.

XI. Jesus is nailed to the Cross.

XII. Jesus dies on the Cross.

XIII. The body of Jesus is taken down from the Cross.

XIV. Jesus is laid in the tomb.

Fast

The current norms for fasting on Good Friday are to take one meatless meal, and if necessary, two smaller meals may be consumed that combined equal less than a full meal. Liquids are allowed at any time, but no food should be eaten between meals. Additional fasting can include refraining from TV, internet, music, and movies.

Take Time for Silence

Try having an afternoon of quiet rest between noon and 3 p.m. Scripture tells us that Jesus was placed on the Cross at 9 a.m., and darkness covered the land from noon until Jesus's death at 3 p.m. (Mk 15:25, 33–38).

Have a Tenebrae Service

Tenebrae in its Latin root refers to shadows and darkness and provides an extended meditation on the Passion and death of Jesus. During that service, candles are extinguished one by one until the final candle is carried away and placed behind a curtain as a symbol of the burial of the Lord. A thunderous noise is made to mark the death of the one who loved beyond all telling. Participants then depart in silence.

Place seven candles on a table with a piece of purple cloth, a cross, or an icon of the Crucifixion or the entombment of Jesus.

> **LEADER:** *Grace to you and peace from God our Father and the Lord Jesus Christ.*
> **RESPONSE:** *Amen.*
> **LEADER:** *Blessed be the name of the Lord our God,*
> **RESPONSE:** *Who redeems us from sin and death.*
> **LEADER:** *For us and for our salvation, Christ became obedient unto death, even death on the Cross.*
> **RESPONSE:** *Blessed be the name of the Lord.*

Read Mark 15 (the NRSVCE version has six paragraphs). After each paragraph, extinguish one candle. Do this until there is only one candle left and just a bit of light in the room. Sit in the shadows for a few minutes and ponder the faithfulness of Jesus in the face of his agony and death.

With the one remaining candle lit, prayerfully read the end of Mark 15 about the burial of Jesus. Then with exuberance, pray the Litany of the Light:

> **LEADER:** *Let us make this Litany of the Light, recalling Jesus, our hope in all things. We make our response:*
> **RESPONSE:** *Christ be our Light.*
> *In these days of shadows and darkness . . .*
> **RESPONSE:** *Christ be our Light. (Continue this response for each line below.)*
> **LEADER:** *For our sisters and brothers who are sick and struggling . . .*
> *In my doubt and in my worry . . .*
> *In moments when hope eludes me . . .*
> *When we fear for those we love . . .*
> *When we dread the darkness of nightfall . . .*
> *When sleep will not come and our hearts are anxious . . .*
> *When morning breaks and we enter a new day . . .*
> *When we are needed by family and friends . . .*
> *When we are called to love without counting the cost . . .*
> *When the crosses we bear seem more than we can carry . . .*
> **ALL:** *Lord Jesus, Light in our darkness, disperse the shadows that surround your people. Renew within us this Holy Week, the light of your grace, that together we may complete this journey of passion with you to rise to a new and everlasting life. Amen.*
> *With Christ as our Light, we are called to shine away shadows and darkness.*[1]

HOLY SATURDAY

A holy day of waiting. Jesus descends into hell to bring to heaven the faithful souls who died before his Passion on the Cross. It's a good time to remember our loved ones who have died and also those who are grieving.

Reach Out to Someone Grieving

Try reaching out to someone who has lost a loved one in the past year and offer your support.

Remember the Women in Your Life

It was the women who remained at the Cross. It was the women who watched where Jesus was taken to be buried and rushed to prepare oils and spices for a proper burial. It was the women who wrapped Jesus's body in the white linens. It was the women who first discovered that the tomb was empty. Think about the women in your own life who have walked with you along your own journey. Say a prayer for each of them.

Dye Easter Eggs with Natural Dyes

Rather than buy the box sets of dye, use natural dyes that you have at home. You can use things like turmeric, red onion, black tea, red cabbage, beets, and yellow onion. You will also need white vinegar and water. You can search online for different dye recipes based on what you have on hand.

Go to Easter Vigil

If you have never been to an Easter Vigil Mass, it is a glorious celebration as we await and then celebrate the Resurrection of Jesus. Many new members of the Church are baptized and confirmed at this Mass. It is rich with meaning and the perfect way to ring in Easter.

easter

A CENTER OF THE LITURGICAL YEAR,
A CELEBRATION OF JESUS'S RESURRECTION

FIFTY DAYS ENDING ON PENTECOST

EASTER

We are an Easter people and Alleluia is our song.
—St. John Paul II

I vividly remember a Holy Week and Easter when I was living in Los Angeles. I had just gone through a breakup, and while in hindsight it feels silly, at the time it was devastating to me. What felt even sadder than the ending of the relationship was the ending of the hope that I had met someone to start a family with. I remember feeling like I could unite my suffering with the crucified Christ, and I felt like I was connected with all of those suffering in the world at the time. But then, two days later, Easter came, and I was presented with the risen Christ. He showed light in the darkness. He rolled away the tomb. He reminded the world that all was not lost, that new life comes, that death does not have the last word.

It was a profound moment as I learned to see that the cycle of life, death, and resurrection does not only happen to Jesus. It happens in the natural world around us, in our bodies, and in the experiences of our lives. Leaves fall off trees, trees lie dormant in cold winter months, new leaves begin to sprout as the earth thaws, and trees are once again lush with blossoms. We can often feel like the disciples on Good Friday—helpless and hopeless. But as Christians, we are called to live in the light of the Resurrection. We know that Easter comes. We know that hope is not lost.

Around us, we can see new life blooming. We, too, are called to new life. We welcome God into the open spaces that have been created from fasting and prayer during Lent. We proclaim, "Hallelujah! Christ is risen!" The joyful day of Christ's Resurrection is here, and the liturgy reflects it with joyous music and decor.

Like Christmas, Easter is not just one day but a whole season. It is known as "Eastertide" and lasts for fifty days, ending with Pentecost Sunday. The season is known for light and renewal and should be lived in joy. Just as we lived a time of quiet contemplation during Lent, we should live the Easter season in celebratory joy.

I have found over the last ten years of my life that having a strong faith community is so important in reminding me that new life is on the other side of death. We aren't meant to walk this journey alone, and we need to hold each other up. Practically, this looks like sending an encouraging text or voice message to a friend you know needs a boost. Maybe it looks like sending a friend ten dollars for a coffee when I know she is having a hard time. It also looks like my friend dropping off a smoothie when she knew I was exhausted from having sick kids for weeks on end. It looks like flowers and phone calls, meals and coffee.

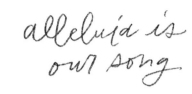

alleluia is
our song

DURING THE EASTER SEASON

Learn the Ancient Call-and-Response of the Easter Season

In early Christianity, the customary Easter greeting was to say to a fellow Christian in joy: "Christ is risen!" And the response would be: "He is risen indeed!" We continue to practice this ancient call-and-response today throughout the Easter season, but especially on Easter Sunday.

Learn to say this classic Easter greeting in a different language.

GREEK
Christos Anesti!
Alithos Anesti!

LATIN
Christus resurrexit!
Vere resurrexit!

ARABIC
Al Masih Kam! (ﺍﻟﻤﺴﻴﺢ ﻗﺎﻡ)
Hakkan kam! (ﺣﻘﺎً ﻗﺎﻡ)

SPANISH
¡Cristo ha resucitado!
¡Verdaderamente ha resucitado!

Restore Thrifted Vases

* Vases from thrift stores
* Spray paint in various colors
* Paint respirator mask
* Newspapers

Thrift some vases from yard sales, the thrift store, or even what is around your house. Pay more attention to the shape of the vase than what is on it. Wash and dry thoroughly. Outdoors or in a well-ventilated space, line your workspace with newspapers to protect the floor. While wearing a mask, grab some spray paint and paint the vases. Let dry.

Fill the vases with springtime flowers—especially Easter lilies. These old vases are given new life!

Make an Easter Tree

* Sticks or willow branches
* Large vase
* Blank egg ornaments or spun cotton eggs
* Acrylic paint
* Paintbrushes

Germans decorate tree branches for Easter with painted eggs. Find some branches in your yard or get willow branches, and put them in a vase. You can purchase blank egg ornaments or spun cotton eggs and paint them with acrylic paint. Leave the Easter tree up for the entire Easter season.

Make Cascarones

* Fresh eggs
* Knife
* Egg dye or paint kit
* Confetti
* Funnel
* Glue
* Tissue paper

Cascarones are a Mexican tradition. With a small knife or needle, cut a hole at the base of each egg and let the yolk and egg white drain out. Rinse the inside of the eggs and let them dry. Dye or paint the eggs like regular Easter eggs. Use a funnel to fill them with confetti. Use glue and tissue paper to close up the other side. It is a lot of work to make them, so you can also purchase them online.

On Easter Sunday, during the Easter egg hunt, everyone can try to crack the cascarones on each other's heads.

DIVINE MERCY SUNDAY

The second Sunday after Easter was designated Divine Mercy Sunday in 2000 by St. John Paul II on the day he canonized St. Faustina Kowalska, a Polish religious mystic famous for her vision of Jesus. In this vision, Jesus revealed the sacred Divine Mercy image, where red and white rays shine from Jesus's heart. On this day, we recall our great need for the divine mercy of God and gratefulness for the mercy already shown us.

ST. FAUSTINA KOWALSKA

OCTOBER 8

Born 1905 in Głogowiec, Russian Empire (modern-day Poland)
Died 1938 in Kraków, Poland

PATRON SAINT OF: Mercy

Pray the Chaplet of Divine Mercy

In her diary, St. Faustina describes a vision where Jesus told her, "I desire to grant unimaginable graces to those souls who trust in My mercy," and he encouraged souls to say the Chaplet of Divine Mercy.[1] You can use your rosary beads to pray it. The full version takes about sixteen minutes, but you can also pray a shortened version, like the one here.

> **SIMPLIFIED DIVINE MERCY CHAPLET**
>
> *Eternal Father, I offer you the Body and Blood, soul and divinity of your dearly beloved Son, our Lord, Jesus Christ, in atonement for our sins and those of the whole world. For the sake of his sorrowful Passion, have mercy on us and on the whole world. (x10)*
>
> *Holy God, Holy Mighty One, Holy Immortal One, have mercy on us and on the whole world. (x3)*
>
> *Jesus, I trust in you. (x3)*

Make a Divine Mercy Sundae

* Vanilla ice cream
* Blue sprinkles or blueberries
* Red sprinkles or strawberry sauce
* Strawberry on top

Scoop some vanilla ice cream and add the red and blue toppings to make a delicious Divine Mercy ice cream sundae.

Dress in Divine Mercy Colors

Wear red, pale blue, or white to represent the rays in the Divine Mercy image.

In St. Faustina's *Diary*, she writes that Jesus said to her, "The two rays denote Blood and Water. The pale ray stands for the Water which makes souls righteous. The red ray stands for the Blood which is the life of souls."[2]

Meditate on the Divine Mercy Image

Make the Divine Mercy image a centerpiece on your dining table or home altar. As you look at the image, think about Jesus's promise that those who venerate it will receive great mercy at the hour of their death: "I promise that the soul that will venerate this image will not perish. I also promise victory over (its) enemies already here on earth, especially at the hour of death. I Myself will defend it as My own glory."[3]

Set an Alarm to Pray

St. Faustina writes that Jesus told her: "At three o'clock, implore My mercy, especially for sinners; and, if only for a brief moment, immerse yourself in My Passion, particularly in My abandonment at the moment of agony.... I will refuse nothing to the soul that makes a request of Me in virtue of My Passion."[4] Set an alarm to pray at 3 p.m. today or every day.

Make a "Jesus, I Trust in You" Lapel Pin

* "'Jesus, I Trust in You' Lapel Pin" template
* White plastic shrink film
* Colored pencils
* Scissors
* Parchment paper
* Baking sheet
* Tie tack or pin back
* Glue gun
* Hot glue

Using the template as a guide, draw on the see-through shrink film with colored pencils. Cut out the shape. Preheat the oven to 350°F. Line a baking sheet with parchment paper and place shrink film on top. Bake for 2–3 minutes. Once cool, attach the pin back or tie back with hot glue.

JESUS, I TRUST IN YOU

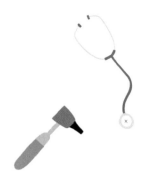

ST. GIANNA MOLLA

APRIL 28

Born 1922 in Magenta, Kingdom of Italy
Died 1962 in Monza, Italy

PATRON SAINT OF: Doctors, mothers, wives, families, unborn

Gianna was a working mother and wife who loved her work as a pediatrician. She died after being given the choice to save her unborn baby's life or her own and choosing her child. She had a strong devotion to Our Lady.

Be Inspired to Pray

> *The stillness of prayer is the most essential condition for fruitful action.*
> —St. Gianna Molla

Write out this phrase and hang it somewhere as a visual reminder to spend fifteen minutes in prayer before you begin your daily tasks. You can write it on a sticky note, practice your calligraphy, or print the "Be Inspired to Pray" template to hang in your home.

Support a Working Mother

Gianna continued to work as a pediatrician once she had children. Working both inside and outside of the home is challenging. Reach out to a working mom friend to see how you can support her. If she says she doesn't need anything, drop off flowers, dinner, or coffee and tell her you are praying for her.

Serve with the St. Vincent de Paul Society

Gianna was a member of the St. Vincent de Paul Society. They have a lot of volunteer opportunities from serving meals to working at their thrift stores. Choose a way to volunteer with them.

THE STILLNESS
OF PRAYER
is the most
essential
condition FOR
FRUITFUL
ACTION.

Saint Gianna Molla

MAY DAY

MAY 1

Catholics have long honored Mary throughout the month of May, most especially with a May Crowning to display her queenship as the mother of Jesus.

Make a "May Day Crowning" Image

* "May Day Crowning" template
* Pencil
* Cardboard piece
* Glue
* Screwdriver
* Flowers

Print out the drawing of Mary. Color the back of the paper with pencil, lay it face up on a piece of cardboard, and then trace the drawing with a heavy hand. When you pull the paper away, you'll have a pencil outline on the cardboard. You can then trace the pencil lines with a marker or paint. To make Mary a crown, poke holes with a screwdriver along her forehead. Fill the holes with flowers.

OUR LADY OF FATIMA

MAY 13

Our Lady of Fatima is a Marian apparition that took place in Fatima, Portugal. She appeared six times to three poor shepherd children between May 13 and October 13 in 1917.

Make Your Own Rosary

Our Lady's main message was to encourage the world to return to prayer, especially through the Rosary, and she issued several warnings that if humanity didn't turn back to God, there would be much world suffering. You can buy rosary kits online, but if you want, you can DIY a rosary from scratch.

* 53 small beads
* 6 larger beads
* Small cross or crucifix charm
* Cord or string
* Scissors
* Craft paint (optional)
* Paintbrushes (optional)

If you want, paint the beads your desired colors and let dry before starting. To begin, string 10 small beads and 1 large bead onto your cord, tying a knot between each bead. Repeat until you have 4 repeats of the pattern, then add another 10 small beads. String both ends of the cord through 1 large bead. Tie a knot, add a small bead, and then tie two knots. Then, add 3 small beads with a knot between each, add two knots after, and string on a large bead. Finally, add your cross charm: feed the cords through the charm's hanging loop in opposite directions so you can tie another knot between the last large bead and the cross. Trim the ends. Use it to pray the Rosary! If you made a rosary accordion box (p. 24), you can store your rosary inside.

Pray for Peace in Our World

Our Lady of Fatima revealed herself as the "Angel of Peace." Think about all of the turmoil that you know between different groups—political, religious, geopolitical—and pray for true peace to be found.

Brew Sun Tea

On Our Lady of Fatima's final appearance, many miracles occurred, including the sun dancing, which was witnessed by thousands of people. Brew sun tea and enjoy a cold glass with lemon.

Dance like the Sun

Have a dance party by yourself, with friends, or with your family.

Make a Sun Print

* Sun print kit
* Leaves and flowers

Purchase a sun print or cyanotype kit and see how the sun leaves images of the leaves and flowers on the paper.

THE ASCENSION

The Ascension is when Jesus ascended to heaven and told his followers that they would receive the gift of the Holy Spirit.

Fly a Kite

You can buy and fly a kite if it's a windy day. Or if it's not so windy, you can make a kite out of fabric and wooden dowels to hang up as a reminder that Jesus ascended into heaven.

Gaze at the Clouds

Lie in your yard or a local park and look up at the sky. Watch the clouds go by and meditate on God, the Creator of the universe.

Go on a Hike

Ascend a mountain or hill nearby. If you have a priest friend who can come along, prepare to have Mass at the top before descending!

Enjoy Meringue

Make or buy things made with meringue! Some ideas are meringue cloud cookies, meringue-topped cake, or lemon meringue pie.

ST. JOAN OF ARC

MAY 30

Born 1412 in Domrémy, Kingdom of France
Died 1431 in Rouen, English-occupied France

PATRON SAINT OF: France

St. Joan was twelve years old when God began giving her visions, eventually asking her to help unite France and make Charles VII the rightful king. Despite much tormenting and ridicule, she was able to convince Charles VII to send her into battle during the Hundred Years War, which brought France multiple victories, led to the formal crowning of Charles VII as foretold in her visions, and eventually helped turn the tide for France to be completely sovereign from England. She was later put on trial for heresy, witchcraft, and dressing like a man. When she refused to lie about her faith in God to save herself, she was burned at the stake at age nineteen. Her martyrdom only inspired the people of France all the more and eventually led to their complete freedom from the English.

Make a Fleur-de-Lis Pennant

St. Joan carried a flag that had the fleur-de-lis symbol on it. The stylized lily represented the French monarchy. When St. Joan marched against the English, she carried her flag to represent God's blessing on her homeland. Later, the three petals of the fleur-de-lis came to represent the Holy Trinity. Make this pennant to remember that God fulfills his promises, as he did to St. Joan.

* "Fleur-de-Lis pennant" template
* Fabric scissors
* Cream felt
* Mustard/gold felt
* Felt glue

Use the template to cut the fleur-de-lis from the gold felt. Cut the cream felt into a pennant shape. Use scraps of gold felt to line and add ties to the left edge of the pennant; affix with felt glue. Glue the fleur-de-lis pieces in the center of the pennant.

Make a Jhesus, Maria Banner

* "*Jhesus, Maria*" template
* Banner, 10 x 12 inches (buy a blank one or sew your own)
* Fabric markers
* Pencil

"Jhesus, Maria" was St. Joan's motto, and it was also written on her flag. Use the template to trace out the letters on the banner with pencil. If you want to try your hand at faux calligraphy, try to letter the words onto the banner freehand: for the downstrokes of the letters, outline thick lines; for the upstrokes, outline thin lines. Fill in the lines with the fabric marker.

jhesus,
maria

Enjoy Some French Delicacies

Eat some French croissants or baguettes, or make savory crepes for dinner.

Write Letters to Soldiers

Write letters through Soldiers' Angels. This charity sends care packages, letters, and cards to support and encourage soldiers and veterans who wouldn't otherwise get mail.

Step into Your Calling

Joan was very courageous and followed where she felt God called her. Take some time to reflect on your own callings.

* What do you think God is calling you to that you are afraid of?
* What is the first step that you could take to step into that calling?
* What are the feelings that come up for you when you think about doing it? Are you afraid, excited, intimidated?
* Invite God into whatever it is that you are feeling and ask for the courage and resolve to do it.

THE VISITATION

MAY 31

Mary, pregnant with Jesus, visited her cousin Elizabeth, who was pregnant with John the Baptist. The words of Elizabeth and Mary during this visit were used to form the Hail Mary prayer.

Pray a Hail Mary (Slowly)

The Hail Mary is a prayer that can be easy to rush through when it is said often. When Elizabeth sees Mary, she is filled with the Holy Spirit and says, "Blessed are you among women, and blessed is the fruit of your womb!" Her exclamation is known as the first devotion to Mary, and it is where we find the words for our own devotions to the Mother of God.

Pray a Hail Mary slowly today. Write down the words in your journal. Draw what these words mean to you. Really dwell on and sit with the meaning and beauty of these words.

Hail, Mary, full of grace,
the Lord is with you.
Blessed are you among women
and blessed is the fruit of your womb, Jesus.
Holy Mary, Mother of God,
pray for us sinners,
now and at the hour of our death.
Amen.

Reflect on God's Promises over Your Life

> *Blessed is she who believed that there would be a fulfillment of what was spoken to*
> *her by the Lord.*
> *—Luke 1:45*

It can be hard to believe in God's promises. What are some of the promises God has made over your life? In what ways have they been fulfilled? Are there some that still have yet to be fulfilled? What are some ways your heart is still longing and yearning?

Write these thoughts down, and pray a Hail Mary over each promise. Ask for Mary's help in having faith in God's fulfillment of his promises to you.

Leap for Joy like John the Baptist

When was the last time you *lept* for anything? Go outside and do a big leap of joy (maybe leap a few times). As you are leaping, reflect:

* How do I greet the Lord in my daily life?
* Do I enter into prayer time joyfully?
* How can I be more childlike in my relationship with God?

Pray the Magnificat

Mary's response after Elizabeth exclaimed, "Blessed are you!" is also known as "Mary's Song." It is also called the "Canticle of Mary" or "Magnificat," which is said during every Evening Prayer in the Church's Liturgy of the Hours. Set an alarm to pray the Magnificat this evening at 6 p.m.

My soul proclaims the greatness of the Lord;
my spirit rejoices in God my savior.
For he has looked upon his handmaid's lowliness;
behold, from now on will all ages call me blessed.
The Mighty One has done great things for me,
and holy is his name.

His mercy is from age to age
to those who fear him.
He has shown might with his arm,
dispersed the arrogant of mind and heart.

He has thrown down the rulers from their thrones
but lifted up the lowly.
The hungry he has filled with good things;
and the rich he has sent away empty.

He has helped Israel his servant,
remembering his mercy,
according to his promise to our fathers,
to Abraham and to his descendants forever.
—Luke 1:46–55 (NABRE)

Visit a Pregnant Friend

Bring food with you and ask how you can help a pregnant friend. Maybe it's taking her other children for an hour or giving her a foot massage. If you don't have a friend who is currently pregnant, you could volunteer at a pregnancy care center.

PENTECOST

Pentecost means "fiftieth" in Greek. Pentecost happened exactly fifty days after Easter. It marks the official end of the Easter season.

At Pentecost we celebrate when the Holy Spirit visited Mary, the apostles, and the other followers of Jesus. Jesus had ascended to heaven nine days earlier (this is why we pray a novena for nine days!), and since then, Mary and the other apostles had been praying continuously. On Pentecost, the Holy Spirit came like a strong, driving wind into the room where they were praying. Soon, fire rested on their heads and gave them the gift of being able to speak in different languages and still understand each other. The Holy Spirit also gave the apostles the other gifts they would need to go out and spread the Gospel.

Make a Birthday Cake

It was after Pentecost that Peter, the first pope, was able to preach his first homily and baptize about three thousand new Christians. Pentecost is considered the birthday of the Church because it is when the Spirit sent the apostles out to preach the Good News!

* "Apostles" template
* Scissors
* Toothpicks
* Tape
* 12 birthday candles

Make your favorite kind of cake to enjoy today. Print out the "Apostles" template, preferably in color, and cut out the apostles. Tape each one to the top of a toothpick and place on the cake, facing out. Place a candle behind each apostle, leaving just enough distance that the apostles won't catch fire. When you light the candles, it will look like the flames have landed on their heads. Sing "Happy Birthday" to the Church.

Pray a Novena

A novena is a set of prayers that are prayed over the course of nine days. The first-ever novena began the day Jesus ascended to heaven, when all the apostles, Mary the Mother of God, and many women gathered in the upper room and prayed. It ended nine days later with the fulfillment of the Holy Spirit descending on Pentecost. Like the apostles' prayer, the Novena to the Holy Spirit is traditionally prayed in preparation for Pentecost. Pray this novena and ask the Holy Spirit to enter your life in a special way this year.

Wear Red

Red is the liturgical color for Pentecost. The color red symbolizes the tongues of fire sent upon the apostles by the Holy Spirit.

Pray in a Different Language

All of them were filled with the Holy Spirit and began to speak
in other languages, as the Spirit gave them ability.
—Acts 2:4

Is there a language you've always wanted to speak? What is your family's heritage, and what language would your ancestors have spoken? Find a translation of your favorite prayer in a different language, and practice saying it.

Make a Holy Spirit Dove Clip

* Moldable foam
* Acrylic paint
* Paintbrush
* Glue gun
* Hot glue
* Hair clip

Shape the moldable foam into the form of a bird. Let it dry and then paint a black dot for an eye and orange triangle for the beak. Glue the dove onto a hair clip.

Make Fruit Popsicles

Make popsicles like the ones on page 85 with fresh fruit and fruit juice.

Buy Peonies

Peonies are known as the "Pentecost rose" because they tend to bloom right before Pentecost. Buy some peonies to decorate your home for Pentecost.

Make a "Fruits of the Spirit" Grocery Tote Bag or Tea Towel

* Scrap cardboard
* Blank canvas tote bag or cotton tea towel
* Fabric paint or fabric markers
* Paintbrush

Insert cardboard into the bag (or place behind the tea towel) so the paint doesn't bleed through. Draw 12 fruits on your canvas tote bag or towel. Paint with fabric paint or markers. Let it be a simple reminder of the 12 fruits of the Spirit: charity, joy, peace, patience, kindness, goodness, generosity, gentleness, faithfulness, modesty, self-control, chastity.

ordinary time

CELEBRATING THE
MYSTERY OF JESUS'S LIFE

ORDINARY TIME II,
THE DAY AFTER PENTECOST
UP TO THE FIRST SUNDAY
OF ADVENT

ORDINARY TIME II

Christ has no body on earth but yours.
Yours are the eyes with which he looks compassionately
on this world. Yours are the feet with which he walks to
do good. Yours are the hands with which he blesses
all the world. Christ has no body now on earth but yours!
—St. Teresa of Avila

It was Pope Benedict XVI who reminded us that Christianity is not a self-help program. Christianity is not *only* about our own personal growth and personal communion with God. In communion with God, we are called to be for the other. Our spiritual lives and our faith should bear fruit and gifts that the Spirit bestowed at Pentecost. If they do not, we must ask Jesus to till our hearts further.

I admit that I am naturally a glass-half-empty kind of woman. I recall a homily given by my spiritual director five years ago where he wondered why many of us are quick to think of all the worst-case scenarios that could happen in our lives and slow to think of all the ways things could go even better than we could ever imagine. Ah, that resonated with me. I am so quick to lose trust in God's goodness for my life. I am so quick to conjure up a narrative of devastation. But when I center myself in prayer, when I look to God to light my way, when I ask the Holy Spirit to move in my life, I can trust that Love carries me and he carries you.

Jesus asks us to be his hands, his feet, and his heart—to be Love for others. We are asked, in this ordinary time, to be for each other. In a world that feels evermore hostile, we as Christians are called to bring kindness and charity, to bring peace and joy, to bring hope and light.

May we ask the Spirit to fill our homes and our lives and spill over into our care for our world and our neighbor.

Christ has no
body on earth
but yours

TRINITY SUNDAY

On the first Sunday after Pentecost, we celebrate the Holy Trinity and honor God, three in one: Father, Son, and Holy Spirit.

Play an Instrument

St. Ignatius of Loyola said the Trinity was like a harmonic chord. "Each key having its own individual sound, but when played together, each key, without losing any of its own distinctiveness, contributes itself and together they form a unified harmonic chord."[1] Play an instrument to celebrate the Trinity today.

Eat Pretzels

Pretzels originated in a monastery in France or Italy when the leftover bread dough was twisted into the shape of crossed arms in prayer. Buy or make pretzels to enjoy while reflecting on the Holy Trinity.

Invite Friends Over

We learn in the Trinity that God is not alone and is brought to fullness in communion with others. We too need community. Invite friends over for dinner, a game night, or maybe even to make pretzels.

Plant Some Pansies

Pansies are sometimes called the "Trinity flower" because of their three colorful petals. Plant these flowers to recall the love and unity of the Holy Trinity.

Make a Trinity Wall Hanging

* "Trinity Wall Hanging" template
* Salt dough or air-dry clay
* Straw
* Clay tools
* Acrylic paint
* Paintbrush
* String

Make salt dough (or use air-dry clay) and roll it flat. Cut out a rainbow arch shape, a cross, and a dove to represent Father, Son, and Holy Spirit. You can print and trace our template if you don't want to draw freehand. Use a straw to make holes on the top and bottom of the arch and cross and just the top of the dove. Dry the dough or clay (anywhere from one day to a week) or bake for a few hours. Once dry and cooled, paint the shapes, then string them together before hanging on a wall.

CORPUS CHRISTI

On this Solemnity of the Most Holy Body and Blood of Christ, we honor the gift of the Eucharist and the mystery of Jesus's presence in the bread and wine. This solemnity is celebrated either on the Thursday or the Sunday following Trinity Sunday.

Attend Eucharistic Adoration or a Procession

Many Catholic parishes will have Eucharistic Adoration and/or a Eucharistic procession in honor of the Solemnity of Corpus Christi. Find out what is happening at the nearby Catholic churches and take part.

Make Bread and Read John 6

Make or buy some sourdough bread from a local bakery. Read the Bread of Life discourse from the Gospel of John (6:22–59).

Decorate with Field Daisies

Daisies are called the "Corpus Christi flower" because they look like monstrances. Decorate your home with field daisies for Corpus Christi.

Make Ribbon Dancers

If we truly understood the Mass, we would die of joy.
—St. John Vianney

* 3 long strips of colorful ribbon
* 3 jingle bells
* Dowel rod
* Glue gun
* Hot glue

String a long piece of ribbon through a bell so that the bell is in the middle of your piece of ribbon. Dab a dot of hot glue near the top of the dowel and attach the center of the ribbon, bell facing out. Knot the ribbon around the dowel. Repeat twice more.

Listen to joyful music and dance around. You can also take these to the Eucharistic procession.

Make Monstrance Art

* Paper, 8 ½ x 11 inches
* Rectangular piece of cardboard a little smaller than the paper
* Cardboard to cut into shapes
* Scrap cardboard
* Scissors
* Glue stick
* Tempera or acrylic paints in gold and yellow
* Rubber brayer

Cut your cardboard: 1 circle 5–10 inches in diameter, plus skinny rectangles 2–5 inches in length and ½–2 inches wide. Glue them onto the larger cardboard piece with the circle in the middle and the rectangles jutting out like sun rays. Squirt some paint on a scrap piece of cardboard and roll the rubber brayer in the paint until it's covered. Roll the rubber brayer onto the cardboard design to cover it in paint. Then print the design onto a piece of paper. You can hang them as home decor, or you could write prayer intentions on the back to take to the adoration chapel to remember who you need to pray for.

Make a Gratitude Journal

It is called: Eucharist, because it is an action of thanksgiving to God.
The Greek words eucharistein *and* eulogein *recall the Jewish blessings that*
proclaim—especially during a meal—God's works: creation, redemption, and
sanctification.
—CCC 1328

* Blank notebook
* Markers or paint and paintbrushes
* Washi tape

Decorate the outside of your notebook with paint or markers and washi tape. Set it out as a reminder to write down 10 things you're grateful for every day until Christmas. If you are married or have roommates, share a notebook to keep each other accountable and share each other's lists. With kids, encourage them to draw pictures of things they are grateful for.

OUR LADY OF AKITA

JUNE 12

Our Lady of Akita is the only approved Asian Marian apparition, which took place from 1973 to 1979 in Yuzawadai, Japan. She appeared three times to Sr. Agnes Katsuko Sasagawa, who was deaf, uniquely through a wooden Marian statue. Our Lady's message was very similar to that of Our Lady of Fatima: encouraging the world to return to prayer, especially through the Rosary, and issuing very severe warnings if humanity didn't turn back to God and repent. Many miracles are attributed to Our Lady of Akita including the healing of Sr. Sasagawa's hearing, the statue bleeding from a wound in its hand, and the statue crying 101 times over the course of eight years, witnessed by many because it was televised in Japan.

Pray the Fatima Prayer

Our Lady of Akita taught Sr. Sasagawa the Fatima Prayer and asked her to recite it after every decade of the Rosary and to get her community to pray it as well. This prayer was not well known in Japan at the time. Pray the prayer as follows:

O my Jesus, forgive us our sins, save us from the fires of hell, and lead all souls to heaven, especially those most in need of your mercy. Amen.

Eat Japanese Food

There are many different kinds of Japanese food you can try. You could get takeout or go to a restaurant. Look to see if you have a ramen restaurant in your area and, if not, find a recipe online. If you're really tight on time, you can buy the quick packs at the store, but then add lots of toppings—hard-boiled eggs, meat, chives, pickled onions, and more! Or enjoy sushi! If you're really adventurous, go to a local Asian mart and get the ingredients to make your own!

SACRED HEART OF JESUS

On the Solemnity of the Sacred Heart, we honor Jesus's inexhaustible divine and human love for God and the world. Celebrated nineteen days after Pentecost, this feast always falls on the Friday after Corpus Christi. Jesus himself requested the celebration of this feast through private revelations to St. Margaret Mary Alacoque of France in 1675.

The Sacred Heart is depicted as a red heart (representing Jesus's divine and human nature united) encircled by a crown of thorns and pierced in its side (Christ's Passion) with droplets of blood coming from the wound (Blood of the Lamb). There are flames at the top (the intense warmth of Jesus's love), a cross (ultimate demonstration of his love for us), and light bursting forth (Light of the World).

Sacred Heart of Jesus, I believe in your love for me.

Create a Matchbox Shrine

* Empty matchbox
* Scissors
* Small piece of cardboard
* Tissue paper
* Mod Podge
* Foam brush
* Picture of the Sacred Heart
* Glitter
* Plastic gems
* Glue

Cut out an oval window from the top of the matchbox. Cover the inside and outside of the matchbox all in tissue paper and Mod Podge. Cut out a piece of cardboard in the form of flames to decorate the top edge of the box. Then paint the whole thing. Glue an image of the Sacred Heart inside of the box and decorate the box with glitter and gems. You can put this on a bookshelf or side table to keep this devotion close.

Pray for the Reunion of Divided Families

Whether it's the brokenness in your own family or that of someone you know, Jesus promises to heal it through devotion to his Sacred Heart and that he will bring peace to families. Write out one way you hope to see healing and peace in your family or the family of someone you love. Pray for that intention.

Rest Your Head on Jesus's Heart

The first devotion to the heart of Jesus was when St. John the apostle rested his head on the breast of Jesus at the Last Supper. Make a Sacred Heart pillowcase so you can rest your head on Jesus's heart.

* "Sacred Heart Pillow Stamp" template
* Pencil
* Thick block rubber erasers
* X-Acto knife
* Fabric paints in red and orange
* Foam brush
* Blank pillowcase
* Cardboard scraps

To make the fabric stamps, use a pencil and the printed template to trace the heart and flame shapes onto a thick block eraser. Place the eraser on a firm surface and use the X-Acto knife to carefully cut away the space around the design; cut small portions at a time, keeping your fingers away from the knife and the direction you are cutting. Cut out the design in the top half of the eraser so you can get a clear impression when you stamp. Place a cardboard scrap inside the pillowcase to prevent the paint from bleeding through. On another cardboard scrap, add a few dollops of red and orange fabric paint. Paint the stamp with fabric paint, then quickly stamp the Sacred Heart image onto the pillowcase, repeating to scatter the image around, and let dry.

IMMACULATE HEART

But Mary treasured all these words and pondered them in her heart.
—Luke 2:19

We can approach Jesus through the Immaculate Heart of Mary. The Feast of the Immaculate Heart of Mary is celebrated as a twin feast on the day after the Sacred Heart of Jesus. The Immaculate Heart of Mary is depicted as a human heart crowned in flames (representing the intense warmth of Mary's love for God and us), pierced by a sword (from Simeon's prophecy in Luke 2:35 that Mary's heart will be pierced by her son's redemptive suffering), and wreathed in roses (sweetness of her maternal care) that are white (purity). Often the heart is depicted with a cross-topped *M* that is Mary's initial.

Prayerfully Contemplate Mary's Immaculate Heart

Read the following prayer as you contemplate Mary's Immaculate Heart:

O Immaculate Heart of Mary, full of goodness, show your love toward us. Let the flame of your heart, O Mary, descend on all people. We love you immensely. Impress true love in our hearts so that we have a continuous desire for your son.

O Mary, gentle and humble of heart, teach us to be more like you—entirely oriented to your son's own heart. Give us, by means of your Immaculate Heart, spiritual health. Let us always see the goodness of your motherly heart, and may we be converted by means of the flame of your heart. Amen.

Decorate Heart-Shaped Cookies with Flowers

Make heart-shaped cookies with icing. Sprinkle them with edible flowers to represent the hearts on the Immaculate Heart image. Then share them with friends.

Create a Mini Shrine to the Immaculate Heart of Mary

* Tin box
* "Immaculate Heart" template
* Magazines
* Scissors
* Glue
* Felt (optional)
* Pom-poms (optional)
* Trinkets such as flowers or religious medals

Cut out images from magazines or various textures such as felt or pom-poms to decorate the inside of the tin box and then glue them to the box. Add the image of the Immaculate Heart of Mary from the printed template and any other trinkets that you have.

STS. ZÉLIE AND LOUIS MARTIN

JULY 12

LOUIS, THE WATCHMAKER

Born 1823 in Bordeaux, Kingdom of France
Died 1894 in Arnières-sur-Iton, France

ZÉLIE, THE LACEMAKER

Born 1831 in Saint-Denis-sur-Sarthon, Kingdom of France
Died 1877 in Alençon, France

PATRON SAINTS OF: Illness, marriage, parenting, widowers, infertility, and child loss

Sts. Azélie-Marie ("Zélie") and Louis Martin were the first married couple to be canonized at the same time. They were parents to St. Thérèse of Lisieux and eight other children. Three of their children passed away within their first year of life, and they lost another at age five. They raised their family and worked together in Zélie's successful lacemaking business until Zélie passed away at age forty-six from breast cancer, when her youngest, Thérèse, was only four years old. All of their surviving children became nuns.

Wear a Watch

Louis was a watchmaker. Wear a watch, and when you look at it throughout the day, pray for those who are struggling in their marriages.

Donate to the Breast Cancer Foundation

Zélie died from breast cancer at the young age of forty-six. Donate in her honor.

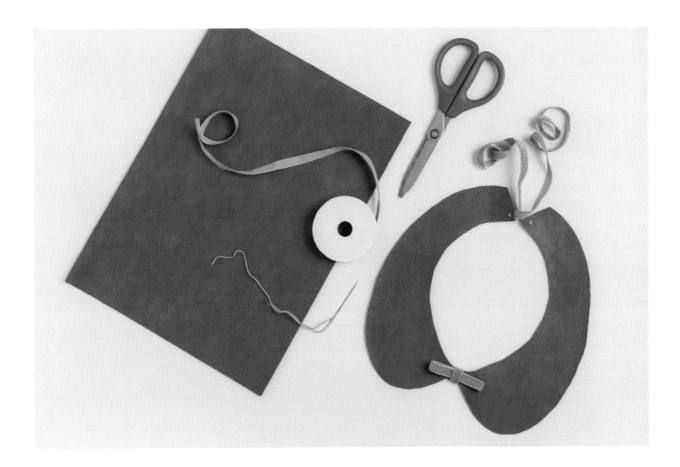

Sew a Removable Collar

Zélie was a well-known lacemaker and owned her own business. She is often depicted wearing a large collar. There are a lot of different ways to make removable collars that you can find online. Here's one to try.

* "Collar" template
* Faux leather, or foam sheets if you're doing it with children
* Scissors
* Velvet ribbon
* Thread
* Needle

Use the template to cut the collar out of your faux leather or foam sheets. Sew a piece of velvet ribbon onto one end of each piece. Then take another piece of velvet ribbon, wrap it around the other ends of the connecting pieces in the form of a bow and sew in place.

Shop Small

The Martins were small-business owners. Buy something from one of your favorite local businesses, or share on social media about one of your favorite small businesses, including what you love about them and your favorite product from them.

Be Intentional about Showing Love to Your Spouse

If you're married, look into love languages and try to figure out which ones resonate with you and with your spouse. According to the theory of the five love languages, we all have two languages that communicate love to us and two by which we love others. The languages include physical affection, words of affirmation, acts of service, quality time, and gifts. Once you know your "languages," act in accordance with your spouse's "languages" to make sure your spouse feels loved today.

PRAYER FOR MARRIAGE

God our Creator,
you drew us together to be companions in life
through the gift of marriage.

May we praise you in our happiness,
seek you in our sorrow, and
find you in our work and need.

Send your Spirit to help us love with vulnerability, intimacy,
*   and joy*
that overflows to serve your people with gratitude and
*   generosity.*

Give us the grace to always see first the goodness in one
*   another*
and to forgive quickly.

And after a happy old age,
together with the circle of our friends and family,
may we come into the fullness of your love
in the kingdom of heaven
through Christ, our Lord.[2]

PRAY FOR YOUR FUTURE SPOUSE

A time when I felt as if God had forgotten me was when my friends all got married and I was still single. It dawned on me that it was likely that my future spouse still had other things he needed to experience before being ready to be in a relationship with me—and I did, too. I began to pray for him—not so much to meet him but for whatever he was going through at that time and that God may be present to him. I also prayed to be open to the ways God was preparing me for him. If you aren't yet married but feel called to marriage, try praying for your future spouse—that God would prepare each of you for your eventual life together and that he would give you patience and perseverance in the meantime.

ST. KATERI TEKAKWITHA

JULY 14

Born 1656 in Ossernenon, USA
Died 1680 in Kahnawake, Canada

PATRON SAINT OF: Native American and First Nations people, integral ecology, the environment

St. Kateri Tekakwitha was the first Native American saint from the territories of what would become the United States and Canada. St. Kateri's father was a Kanien'kehá:ka (Mohawk) chief, and her mother was an Algonquin Catholic. A smallpox epidemic when she was young that took the lives of her parents also left her forever weakened, partially blind, and with scarred skin. At age nineteen, she converted to Christianity and chose to leave her tribe because of increased hostility she experienced because of her faith. She walked two hundred miles (which took her two months) to a nearby Christian town where she lived the rest of her life and became known as the "Lily of the Mohawks." When she died at age twenty-four, witnesses say that Kateri's scars disappeared and her skin shone with a "holy radiance."

Learn How to Pronounce Kateri's Name

The Mohawk pronunciation is *Gaderi Dega'gwita*.

What Her Name Means

Kateri's baptismal name is Catherine, which became "Kateri" in Mohawk.

Kateri's Mohawk name, "Tekakwitha," has many translations, including "one who places things in order" or "one who walks groping for her way," which is a reference to her poor eyesight.

Go to Eucharistic Adoration

Kateri would spend hours or even entire days in Eucharistic Adoration in church, even during the coldest weather in Canada. Make a plan to go to adoration this week, even if it's only for ten minutes.

Support an Organization Founded by Indigenous People

There are many Indigenous communities that are impoverished. Research which tribes inhabited your town and find ways to aid their efforts to self-determination. We recommend St. Joseph Mission School and Tekakwitha Conference.

Make Small Wooden Crosses

When the winter hunting season took Kateri and many of the villagers away from the village, she made her own little chapel in the woods by making a wooden cross and spending time there in prayer, kneeling in the snow.

* 2 sticks for each cross
* Twine or string

Find 2 sticks and tie them together in the shape of a cross with some twine or string. Pray a simple prayer. (Kateri's last words and prayer was "Jesus, I love you.") Make several crosses and leave them around your neighborhood or a nearby natural area for others to find as a delightful surprise.

Play or Watch Lacrosse

Kateri's tribe invented lacrosse! Find videos on YouTube and teach yourself how to play, or simply watch a match.

STS. JOACHIM AND ANNE

JULY 26

PATRON SAINTS OF: Grandparents, infertility

Joachim and Anne are the parents of the Blessed Virgin Mary, and they experienced infertility until becoming pregnant with Mary. They are the grandparents of Jesus.

Call Your Grandparents

Call your grandparents if they are still alive or have your children call their grandparents. If they are local to you, bake cookies and then deliver them and spend time with them. If you are a grandparent, treat yourself to something special today or request to spend time with your grandchildren.

Pray for Your Friends Who Are Experiencing Infertility

It is said that St. Anne was barren until she and Joachim conceived Mary. Pray for your friends who are experiencing infertility today. Send them a spiritual bouquet and tell them you are thinking of them.

What Is a Spiritual Bouquet?

A spiritual bouquet is a collection of prayers, sacrifices, and devotional acts offered as a gift or offering to God, typically given to celebrate a special occasion or to support someone in need of spiritual encouragement. They can be given in various forms, such as a card, letter, certificate, or paper flowers.

A Spiritual Bouquet for you

FOR YOU

STS. MARY, MARTHA, LAZARUS

JULY 29

PATRON SAINTS OF: Siblings

The siblings Mary, Martha, and Lazarus of Bethany are integral in many biblical stories throughout Jesus's ministry. From Jesus reminding Martha not to be anxious about so many things, to praising Mary for her listening presence, to raising Lazarus from the dead, it's clear that these siblings were dear friends of Jesus.

Read Luke 10:38–42 (Martha and Mary) and John 11:1–44 (Raising of Lazarus)

Notice how natural Jesus is with Martha, Mary, and Lazarus. He loves them generously and speaks into their deepest needs. Spend time in prayer and allow Jesus to meet you where you are. What needs do you have today? Ask Jesus to both reveal them and to show you how to fulfill those needs.

Celebrate Your Siblings

* Send an affirmation text or letter to your sibling(s), thanking them for the gifts they bring to the family or how they've influenced you to be the person you are today.
* Start planning a siblings-only trip sometime in the next year.
* Pray for your sibling(s).

Sit with Jesus like Mary of Bethany

Spend some time in silence with Jesus. Read scripture. Meditate. Set a timer for thirty minutes of uninterrupted time.

Be Hospitable like Martha

Invite a friend over for a coffee in the afternoon. Just sit and chat for an hour.

Rise Up like Lazarus

Jesus commanded Lazarus to rise up from his grave. It's a command for each of us: What are the dead parts inside of us that need to rise up like Lazarus?

What is something you've always loved doing but haven't made time for lately? Make a plan to do something you love this week.

Is there a dream God has placed on your heart? Check in with yourself: Is God calling you to let this dream go or does he want to breathe new life into it?

ST. IGNATIUS OF LOYOLA

JULY 31

Born 1491 in Azpeitia, Spain
Died 1556 in Rome, Italy

PATRON SAINT OF: Retreats

The founder of the Jesuits and mystic St. Ignatius of Loyola initially had no intention of being a follower of Christ, preferring military success and fortune. But when he was bedridden after a cannonball shattered his leg, he read the life of Christ and the saints, was deeply moved, and began his long, painful conversion to Christ. Known for writing *Spiritual Exercises,* his spirituality can be summed up in the Jesuit motto, *Ad majorem Dei gloriam*—"For the greater glory of God."

Pray the Suscipe

Take, Lord, and receive all my liberty,
my memory, my understanding,
and my entire will,
All I have and call my own.

You have given all to me.
To you, Lord, I return it.

Everything is yours; do with it what you will.
Give me only your love and your grace,
that is enough for me.

Pray the Daily Examen

Tonight before bed, pray the Examen, a contemplative, memory-guided prayer written by St. Ignatius:

* Give thanks to God for all the ways he has blessed you today.
* Ask for the grace to see where you've sinned today and for the strength to reject your sins.
* Examine the day by reviewing your morning, midday, afternoon, and evening. What were your thoughts, words, and deeds during these times?
* Ask God to forgive you for your sins and shortcomings of the day.
* Out of love for Jesus, determine to do better with the help of the Holy Spirit.

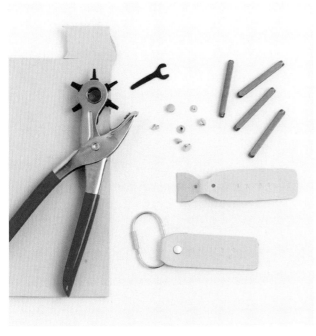
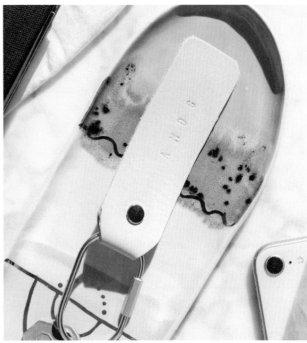

Make an AMDG Keychain

Ad majorem Dei gloriam (For the greater glory of God), or AMDG, is the motto of the Society of Jesus, which Ignatius founded.

* "AMDG Keychain" template
* Leather scraps
* Pen or pencil
* Fabric scissors
* Metal alphabet stamps
* Hammer
* Brass key ring
* Brass rivet
* Leather punch
* Piece of painter's or masking tape

Trace the keychain template on the back of your leather with a pencil. Carefully cut it out. Fold it over the key ring and mark where you want to position your rivet; make sure to mark it on both sides of the fold. Open it up and punch a hole on both sides with your leather punch. Fold it over around the key ring, then screw in the rivet. Grab the letters *A*, *M*, *D*, and *G* from your metal stamps and a hammer. Place the piece of tape along the line where you want your letters to align. If you want them to be exact, you can measure the spaces out and mark with a pencil. Place your letters on the leather and hammer to indent it.

Have a Cannonball Contest

Ignatius talked about his "cannonball moment" when his whole life changed. Have a cannonball contest at the swimming pool!

TRANSFIGURATION

AUGUST 6

On the Feast of the Transfiguration, we commemorate when Jesus took three of his disciples—Peter, James, and John—up on a mountain to pray. Moses and Elijah appeared, and Jesus was transfigured to show his divinity and glory, with his face and clothes becoming dazzlingly bright. The disciples made three tents for Moses, Elijah, and Jesus. Read about the Transfiguration in Mark 9:2–13; Matthew 17:1–13; and Luke 9:28–36.

Eat Grapes

Growing grapes on a vine is a natural transfiguration. The grapes begin as a seed, develop into a bud, then a flower, and then ripen into fruit. The grapes can be crushed into juice, which can be turned into wine and eventually the Blood of Christ in the Eucharist. Traditionally grapes are blessed on the Feast of the Transfiguration.

Today, eat grapes, grape jelly, or grape popsicles. Enjoy a glass of wine with friends or your significant other.

Hike a Mountain

Jesus took the apostles Peter, James, and John on top of Mount Tabor where he was then transfigured. Enjoy a nice hike on a hill or mountain, and reflect on the glory of God.

Make Three Tents

Make tents out of blankets and furniture. Read in them, watch a movie, or even spend time in prayer. Ask God to transform your heart.

Make a Butterfly Garden

The Transfiguration is referred to as Metamorphosis in the Eastern Church. Set up a butterfly garden with caterpillars and watch them transform.

ST. MAXIMILIAN KOLBE

AUGUST 14

Born 1894 in Zduńska Wola, Poland
Died 1941 in Auschwitz-Birkenau concentration camp, German-occupied Poland

PATRON SAINT OF: Addicts, those recovering from addiction, prisoners, families

St. Maximilian Kolbe is known for his intense devotion to Mary, his dedication to rid the world of religious indifference, and his martyrdom. While he was imprisoned in the Nazi camp of Auschwitz, he offered himself up in exchange for the life of a fellow prisoner who had a wife and two sons.

Write Letters to a Prisoner

St. Maximilian Kolbe died in a concentration camp when he told the Nazis to take *his* life instead of the life of another man who had a wife and children. This man whose life was spared was even able to attend Maximilian's canonization! Write letters to a prisoner; here are some recommended resources:

* The Order of Malta Pen Pal Program: https://orderofmaltaamerican.org/spirituality-in-action/prison /pen-pal/
* Sr. Helen Prejean's guide: sisterhelen.org/writing-to-someone-in-prison-old/
* Send a book to a prisoner: www.pemdc.org/freeresources/prison-ministry/prisoner/

Read and Start Following Journalism

St. Maximilian Kolbe founded Catholic presses and radio stations in Poland. Ask your friends what storytelling platforms they follow or listen to, and try some of them yourself.

Spend Time with Mary

St. Maximilian Kolbe loved Mary. When he was a young boy, he had a vision of her. He told his parents: "I prayed very hard to Our Lady to tell me what would happen to me. She appeared, holding in her hands two crowns, one white, one red. She asked if I would like to have them—one was for purity, the other for martyrdom. I said, 'I choose both.' She smiled and disappeared."[3]

Spend time with Mary by making (p. 140) and praying a Rosary. Or learn how to sing a verse of "Hail, Holy Queen Enthroned Above."

Wear the Miraculous Medal

St. Maximilian Kolbe was in love with Mother Mary and encouraged wearing the Miraculous Medal as a regular reminder of Mary's tender care for us. Look up the history of and photos of Miraculous Medal online.

ASSUMPTION OF MARY

AUGUST 15

On the Feast of the Assumption, we celebrate Mary being lifted up to heaven, body and soul, at the end of her life. The belief that her body avoided the decay of death acknowledges the special role she played in bearing God's Son to us. With her assumption into heaven, she shares in the glory of Jesus's Resurrection and anticipates the resurrection of the body that we all will experience one day.

Make a Cloud Pillow

Envision Mary's assumption into heaven by crafting a heavenly environment on earth. You can make a cloud pillow out of fabric following the instructions for the Mary Pillow (p. 25), but if you are new to sewing, you can make this "learn to sew" project using butcher paper instead!

* White butcher paper
* Hole punch
* Yarn
* Yarn needle
* Stuffing

Cut a cloud shape out of white butcher paper. Punch holes every inch or ¾ inch around the edge. Using a yarn needle, thread the yarn through each hole, back and forth, until you only have a few inches left. Fill with stuffing, then finish sewing the remaining holes and tie the yarn off.

Plant an Herb Garden

Polish folklore connects the Feast of the Assumption with a harvest festival where people bless the fruits of their gardens and celebrate healing properties of herbs. Plant an herb garden indoors or outdoors.

* Rosemary was known as Mary's Bouquet.
* Spearmint was known as Our Lady's Mint.
* Sage was known as Mary's Shawl.

Take a Nap

This feast was known in the seventh century as the "Falling Asleep of the Mother of God" (*Koinesis Theotokou*). Enjoy an afternoon nap.

Make Meringue Treats

I also make meringues to celebrate the Ascension (p. 144), but their cloudlike appearance makes them perfect for the Assumption!

ST. TERESA OF CALCUTTA

SEPTEMBER 5

Born 1910 in present-day Skopje, North Macedonia
Died 1997 in Calcutta, India

PATRON SAINT OF: World Youth Day, Missionaries of Charity, Archdiocese of Calcutta

Fondly known as Mother Teresa, she is globally recognized for her work among the poorest of the poor in India. Born to Albanian parents and originally named Anjezë Gonxhe Bojaxhiu, this soon-to-be saint felt a strong call to serve as a missionary in India. She founded the order called Missionaries of Charity, which continues to be a thriving community worldwide. Her love for the poor and marginalized is an inspiration to serve and find Christ even in those considered unlovable.

Make Blessings Bags for the Homeless

Use a gallon-size resealable plastic bag and include:

nice socks

warm gloves & HotHands (if it's cold where you are) or instant ice packs (if it's hot where you are)

bandages

wet wipes

nail clippers

toothbrush & toothpaste

tuna & cracker packs

individual packages of snacks

water bottle & sunscreen

enough money for one bus ride in your town that they could use to get to a shelter

Keep the bags in your car so that you can hand them out spontaneously when you see a need.

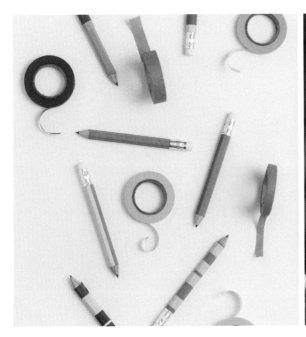

Decorate Pencils

I am like a little pencil in his hand. That is all. He does the thinking.
He does the writing. The pencil has nothing to do with it.
—Mother Teresa

* Pencils
* Washi tape

Decorate pencils with washi tape.

Smile

I think that if we all look into our own homes, how difficult we find it sometimes to smile at each other, and that the smile is the beginning of love. And so let us always meet each other with a smile, for the smile is the beginning of love, and once we begin to love each other naturally we want to do something.

—Mother Teresa

Be cognizant of how much (or little) you smile, and then smile more. Smile at the cashier, smile at your children and spouse, and smile when you don't feel like smiling.[5]

Eat Indian Food

There are lots of delicious curries that are easy to make or order in from a local restaurant. Eat Indian food tonight in honor of Mother Teresa's feast day.

ST. HILDEGARD VON BINGEN

SEPTEMBER 17

Born 1098 in Bermersheim vor der Hoehe, Holy Roman Empire
(present-day Germany)
Died 1179 in Bingen, Germany

PATRON SAINT OF: Musicians, writers

One of only four female Doctors of the Church, St. Hildegard was a mystic, healer, artist, scientist, composer, poet, writer, philosopher, theologian, and German Benedictine abbess. Born to a noble family, she started receiving visions from God when she was three years old, so she always had a special relationship with God and his creation. She wielded the knowledge from her visions to advise emperors and bishops, start a new order, compose poetry and music, author many books, and create healing recipes.

Spend Time in a Garden

> *It is fitting that the rays of the sun should shine upon that root which has been plant-ed by the Holy Spirit, and that a gentle rain should moisten it, for a good field which brings forth good fruit flourishes in the sun and the rain and the dew.*
> *—St. Hildegard von Bingen*

Draw Mandala Circles

Hildegard drew circles and mandalas in her work because they reflect the divine order. Try drawing man-dala circles in her memory.

Reach Out to Someone with Anxiety

Text or call a friend who you know is struggling to see if they want to go on a walk or a hike, get a pedi-cure or massage, or go out for lunch. Give them plenty of space to talk about what's going on while you supportively listen.

Use the Color Green

Hildegard spoke of *viriditas*, which represents both the green color of living things and the idea of vitality. It is a word that reflects physical and spiritual health. She trusted that our bodies have *viriditas*, or "greening power," to heal themselves, and she wrote of many methods to help bring the body back into balance when it is ill.

Use the color green in one of the following ways:

* Paint with the color green. (I took an old framed canvas and painted it green to hang in our house.)
* Eat green vegetables for dinner.
* Spend time in green nature.
* Wear something green.

Eat Foods of Joy

Hildegard received visions of many things from God, including heavenly visions of the healing power of food and the importance of good nutrition for well-being. "Foods of joy" brought revitalization and helped preserve good health in every aspect of our lives: psychological, spiritual, and physical.[6]

Eat foods today that bring you health and joy.

Bake Cookies of Joy

These "cookies of joy" are a recipe against melancholy and depression, wielding together spelt flour, nutmeg, cinnamon, and cloves to "calm all bitterness of the heart and mind, open your heart and impaired senses, and make your mind cheerful."[7]

* 12 tablespoons organic raw butter
* ¾ cup organic brown sugar
* ⅓ cup raw organic honey
* 4 pasture-raised organic egg yolks
* 2½ cups organic spelt flour (ancient grain and key ingredient)
* 1 teaspoon sea salt
* St. Hildegard's "spices that bring joy" mix: 1 tablespoon nutmeg, 1 tablespoon cinnamon, and 1 teaspoon cloves
* Flour for dusting surface

Melt the butter over low heat in a small saucepan. Transfer butter to a medium bowl, then slowly add sugar, honey, and egg yolks, beating lightly. Fold in the rest of the ingredients, gently. Refrigerate the dough for an hour.

Lightly flour a surface and then roll out the cookie dough until about a ¼ inch thick. Cut the dough into small circles using a cookie cutter or drinking glass. Line a baking sheet with parchment paper, place the cookies on top, and then bake at 375°F for 10 minutes or until golden-brown. Let cool, then enjoy.[8]

If you would like to cook St. Hildegard's own recipes, check out the book *From Saint Hildegard's Kitchen: Foods of Health, Foods of Joy* by Jany Fournier-Rosset (Liguori Publications, 2010).

FEAST OF THE ARCHANGELS (MICHAELMAS)

SEPTEMBER 29

ST. MICHAEL

PATRON SAINT OF: Grocers, soldiers, doctors, mariners, paratroopers, police, sickness

ST. GABRIEL

PATRON SAINT OF: Messengers, telecommunication workers, postal workers

ST. RAPHAEL

PATRON SAINT OF: Travelers, the blind, bodily ills, happy meetings, nurses, physicians, medical workers, matchmakers, Christian marriage, Catholic studies

The three archangels are chief messenger angels entrusted by God. St. Michael is a protector, St. Gabriel is a messenger of Good News, and St. Raphael is a healer.

Eat Blackberries

Legend has it that when St. Michael threw Satan out of heaven (Rv 12), the devil landed on a blackberry bush, which he then spit on and cursed.

Bake a cobbler or pie, eat some fresh blackberries, or top some angel food cake with them.

Have a Feast!

The traditional Michaelmas dinner consisted of roasted goose and carrots (typical for the season in Britain). Sometimes the day was also known as "Goose Day," and as an old rhyme said, "Eat a goose on Michaelmas Day, want not for money all the year." Unless you have a goose on hand, consider roasting a chicken with carrots instead!

Deliver Michaelmas Daisy Bouquets

The aster flower is known as the Michaelmas daisy.

The Michaelmas daisies, among dede weeds,
Bloom for St Michael's valorous deeds.
And seems the last of flowers that stood,
Till the feast of St. Simon and St. Jude.[9]

(The Feast of Sts. Simon and Jude is October 28.)

Consider delivering daisies to helpers in your community.

ST. THÉRÈSE OF LISIEUX

OCTOBER 1

Born 1873 in Alençon, France
Died 1897 in Lisieux, France

PATRON SAINT OF: Florists, missionaries, pilots, priests

The youngest daughter of Sts. Zélie and Louis Martin, St. Thérèse became a cloistered Carmelite nun in Lisieux, France, at age fifteen. She struggled painfully yet quietly with tuberculosis until her death at age twenty-four. Her "little way" of making small, quiet sacrifices with love reminds us that sainthood is achievable each time we allow God to draw us out of ourselves.

Make Little Food

Make little food (see p. 10 from Mary's baby shower) in honor of St. Thérèse's "little way" or deliver flower bouquets (see p. 206).

Spend Time with Flowers

St. Thérèse loved nature and often used nature imagery to describe God's abiding love. She is known as "the Little Flower" because she saw the ways small wildflowers grew in forests and fields yet were no less beautiful because they were unnoticed. Rather than a grand lily or elegant rose, she understood herself as a small flower who bloomed where God planted her. She said, "If every flower were a rose, spring would lose its loveliness."

Learn to paint watercolor flowers, work on your garden, or visit a botanical garden.

Make Resin Floral Coasters

* Pictures of St. Thérèse
* Mod Podge
* Dried flowers
* Resin kit
* Coaster mold

Cut out the pictures of St. Thérèse. Cover with Mod Podge on both sides and let them dry so that they become water resistant. Follow the instructions on the resin kit and pour half of the resin into the mold. In each coaster, add a picture of St. Thérèse and arrange the dried flowers around it. Wait a minimum of 4 hours before pouring the rest of the mold. Let it set for 24 hours. Keep her near all year!

Make a Daisy Chain Bracelet

* Size 8/0 seed beads in multiple colors
* 0.8–1 mm silk thread
* Beading needle
* 3 mm round gold beads
* Jewelry closures

Tie a knot at the end of your thread, and thread the other end through the needle. Add seed beads to form a line between your daisies. To make a daisy shape, add 4 beads in the color of the petals and then a yellow or gold bead (this will be the center of the flower). Then pass the needle through the first 4 beads to make a loop; pull the thread through. Then add 4 more beads in the petal color and loop the needle through the yellow bead. Add more beads to separate this daisy from the next, then repeat to make another daisy. When the bracelet is the desired length, tie the jewelry closures on either end of the thread. Wear it and think about how you can be a little flower like St. Thérèse!

Play Ball

I had offered myself to the Child Jesus to be His little plaything. I told Him not to treat me like one of those precious toys which children only look at and dare not touch, but to treat me like a little ball of no value, that could be thrown on the ground, kicked about, pierced, left in a corner, or pressed to His Heart just as it might please Him. In a word, I wished to amuse the Holy Child and let Him play with me as He fancied. Here [In Rome] He was answering my prayer.

—St. Thérèse of Lisieux

St. Thérèse wanted Jesus to use her as a toy, something to love and play with without worrying about breaking it.[10] Play ball today and think about how much fun you have while you kick, hit, or bounce it around. How can you open yourself and bring joy to Jesus like a little ball?

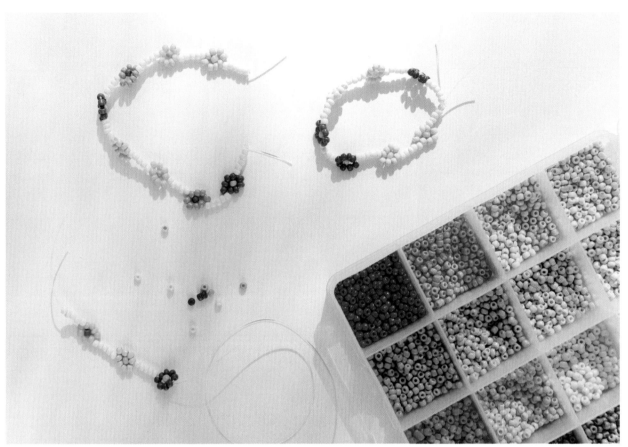

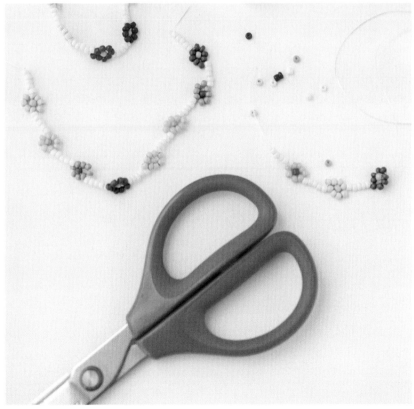

ST. FRANCIS OF ASSISI

OCTOBER 4

Born 1181 in Assisi, Roman Empire
(present-day Italy)
Died 1226 in Assisi, Roman Empire
(present-day Italy)

PATRON SAINT OF: Animals, archaeologists, ecology, Italy, merchants, messengers, metal workers

Born into a noble family, St. Francis had every intention of living forever in luxury until he began receiving visions from God. The most famous vision occurred when Jesus spoke to him through the San Damiano cross at an abandoned church and said, "Go and repair my church which . . . is wholly a ruin."[11] St. Francis renounced all worldly goods and literally began rebuilding the abandoned church, as well as serving the poor and leading a community of brothers and sisters in the Franciscan way. St. Francis of Assisi is known for his radical vows of poverty and his love for the poor.

Spend Time in Nature and Praise God's Creation

St. Francis is the patron saint of ecology. St. Francis loved God's creation and saw all living things as worthy of honor. All creation is precious to God and harmoniously works together for good.

Spend time in nature and praise God's creation in one of the following ways:

*   Do some gardening and dedicate your garden to St. Francis.
*   Go for a walk or hike.

Delight in Animals

St. Francis is also the patron saint of animals. One famous story is how he preached the Word of God to birds, who stood silent and listened until he was finished and didn't leave until he had blessed them.

Delight in animals like St. Francis. Here are some ideas:

* Go bird watching. Notice the beauty in God's most carefree creatures.
* Give your pets some extra-special love. Give them a treat, go for a walk with them, or pray a blessing over them. Call them "Brother" or "Sister" today, like St. Francis would have. Sometimes parishes will have a special animal blessing on St. Francis's feast day.
* Visit an animal shelter to volunteer time.

Make a Bird Feeder Ornament

* 2 envelopes gelatin
* ⅔ cup boiling water
* Bowl
* Spoon
* 2 cups birdseed, more as needed
* Cookie cutters, especially in animal shapes
* String or twine
* Parchment paper
* Baking sheet
* Drinking straw

Set your cookie cutters on parchment paper. Dissolve the gelatin in the bowl of boiling water. Then add the birdseed and continue to stir. If the mixture is runny, add a bit more birdseed. Scoop the mixture into your cookie cutters, pressing as you go to make sure that it's compact. Stick the straw near the top to create a hole, and thread the string through the hole, tying a knot after leaving a loop for hanging. Once dry, pop the ornament out of the cookie cutter. Hang on a branch that is near a place where the birds can perch.

These also make really cute gifts, especially if you attach the printed "Canticle of the Creatures" to them (p. 217).

Bake St. Francis's Favorite Almond Cookies

When St. Francis was on his deathbed, he asked his follower, Bl. Jacoba, to bring him his favorite treat—her almond cookies. Bake and enjoy a batch in honor of St. Francis!

* 1¾ cup whole almonds
* 1 cup sugar
* 2 teaspoon flour
* ⅛ teaspoon salt
* 4 egg whites
* ½ teaspoon almond extract
* ¼ cup sliced almonds

Preheat the oven to 300°F, and line a baking sheet with parchment paper. If you like, toast the whole almonds before you begin by cooking them in a dry frying pan over medium heat, stirring until fragrant. (This makes the cookies even more delicious!) Once cool, process them in a food processor or a spice grinder until until they reach a mealy texture. In a separate bowl, whisk egg whites to loosen them up. Add everything except the sliced almonds, and stir thoroughly until it forms a dough.

Use a teaspoon to scoop the dough onto the baking sheet, leaving at least an inch between the cookies. Decorate with sliced almonds. Bake at 300°F for 25 minutes. Makes about 48 cookies.[13]

Make a Tau Cross

The tau cross is a sign of conversion, which Francis considered essential in the Franciscan way—its unique shape reminds us to turn toward God and toward others. St. Francis used this sign as his personal signature. Use the template to trace the tau cross onto a flattened piece of clay. Use water to smooth out the edges to give it a rounded shape.

Eat Italian

Assisi, the hometown of St. Francis, is located in the Umbria region of Italy. Eat some simple meals common to that area:

* Bruschetta
* Antipasto salad with salami, ham, and pecorino cheese
* Frittata
* Lentil soup
* Polenta
* Fettuccine con la ricotta
* Pasta alla Norcina

Hang the San Damiano Cross

Pray what St. Francis prayed in the crumbling church of San Damiano, and ask the Lord to help you do his will.[12] Hang the San Damiano cross in your home.

Give Up Something Frivolous and Donate the Proceeds

St. Francis came from a wealthy family, but after his conversion experience, he decided to live a life of radical poverty and sold all he had. To this day, many friars and sisters of the Franciscan orders make permanent vows of poverty as part of their initiation into the order.

Give up something luxurious in your day today and donate what you would have spent to a charitable organization.

Pray the "Canticle of the Creatures"

Pray St. Francis's "Canticle of the Creatures" that praises God and celebrates his beautiful creation.

Most High, all-powerful, good Lord,
Yours are the praises, the glory, and the honor, and all blessing,
To You alone, Most High, do they belong,
and no human is worthy to mention Your name.

Praised be You, my Lord, with all Your creatures,
especially Sir Brother Sun,
Who is the day and through whom You give us light.
And he is beautiful and radiant with great splendor;
and bears a likeness of You, Most High One.

Praised be You, my Lord, through Sister Moon and the stars, in
heaven You formed them clear and precious and beautiful.

Praised be You, my Lord, through Brother Wind,
and through the air, cloudy and serene, and every kind of
weather,
through whom You give sustenance to Your creatures.

Praised be You, my Lord, through Sister Water,
who is very useful and humble and precious and chaste.

Praised be You, my Lord, through Brother Fire,
through whom You light the night,
and he is beautiful and playful and robust and strong.

Praised be You, my Lord, through our Sister Mother Earth,
who sustains and governs us,
and who produces various fruit with colored flowers and
herbs.[14]

ST. JOHN PAUL II

OCTOBER 22

Born 1920 in Wadowice, Poland
Died 2005 in the Vatican

PATRON SAINT OF: World Youth Day

Known as Karol Józef Wojtyla or "Lolek" growing up, the soon-to-be pope was no stranger to loss. His mother, father, and older brother all died before his twenty-first birthday. Though he had always wanted to be an actor, Karol later discerned a vocation to the priesthood right when World War II was underway. He organized many secret faith meetings, disguised as outdoor trips, with young Christians hungry to grow in their faith. Elected as the first non-Italian pope in 455 years, St. John Paul II successfully promoted interfaith initiatives, encouraged peace between nations, and created World Youth Day.

Go on a Hike or Go Swimming

St. John Paul II loved sports and especially enjoyed hiking and swimming. Go on a hike, or go swimming if it's warm enough. Connect with God while moving your body.

Practice Forgiveness

When a man shot the pope in an assassination attempt, St. John Paul II visited him in his jail cell and forgave him. He often spoke of forgiveness: "We all need to be forgiven by others, so we must all be ready to forgive. *Asking and granting forgiveness* is something profoundly worthy of every one of us."[15]

Who might you need to ask for forgiveness from or who might you need to forgive (even if they haven't asked you for it)?

Make a "Be Not Afraid" Shirt or Bag

In his first address as pope, St. John Paul II proclaimed the words "Be not afraid!" It became a common phrase that he used throughout his papacy. The phrase is written in the Bible 365 times—one for every day of the year.

Make a T-shirt, pencil pouch, or tote bag with this message.

* "Be Not Afraid" template
* Iron-on paper
* Iron
* Printer
* Items to iron on (T-shirts, canvas pencil pouch, canvas tote bag)

Print the template of St. John Paul II's proclamation onto iron-on paper. Iron it onto a T-shirt, canvas pencil pouch, or canvas tote bag.

Reflect on the World Youth Day Homily

Look up Pope John Paul II's "World Youth Day Homily" online. The text is available in full on the Vatican's website. Reflect on the role that God, your friends, and your family have in your life. Ask yourself if you are leaning more on people or on God. Print and hang up the "World Youth Day Homily" template to remind yourself to put God first.

Around you, you hear all kinds of words. But only Christ speaks words that stand the test of time and remain for all eternity. The time of life that you are living calls for decisive choices on your part: decisions about the direction of your studies, about work, about your role in society and in the Church. It is important to realize that among the many questions surfacing in your minds, the decisive ones are not about "what". The basic question is "who": "who" am I to go to, "who" am I to follow, "to whom" should I entrust my life?

You are thinking about love and the choices it entails, and I imagine that you agree: what is really important in life is the choice of the person who will share it with you. But be careful! Every human person has inevitable limits: even in the most successful of marriages there is always a certain amount of disappointment. So then, dear friends, does not this confirm what we heard the Apostle Peter say? Every human being finds himself sooner or later saying what he said: "To whom shall we go? You have the words of eternal life." Only Jesus of Nazareth, the Son of God and of Mary, the eternal Word of the Father born two thousand years ago at Bethlehem in Judaea, is capable of satisfying the deepest aspirations of the human heart.

ALL SAINTS' DAY

NOVEMBER 1

On this day we honor all saints, canonized or not, known or unknown. Reading the stories of the saints and praying to them reminds us that there are many paths to sainthood, and we are all called to holiness just like they were. All Saints' Day is a holy day of obligation.

Attend Mass

Today is a holy day of obligation.

Make a Punch Needle Saint

* "Black-and-White Saint Images" template
* Iron-on paper
* Iron
* Punch needle
* Golden yarn
* Scissors
* Embroidery hoop
* Punch needle fabric, monk's cloth, or throw pillow cover
* Stuffing for pillow (optional)
* Needle and thread for pillow (optional)

Print out a picture of one of the black-and-white saint images in the template (or one of your favorite saint images from the internet) onto iron-on paper. Cut it out and iron it onto the fabric. Place the fabric facedown in the embroidery hoop (catching only one layer if using a pillow cover), centering the saint's face in the hoop so you can use it as a template for the halo. You can draw the outline of the saint with a pencil if you need some guidance. Thread your punch needle: stick your bent wire from the tip of the needle toward the top. Thread your yarn through the hoop of the wire, then pull the wire out of the tip. Repeat with the tiny hole in the needle tip, leaving a 2-inch tail of yarn.

To start punch needling, stick your needle in your starting point from the front and then look at the backside of your fabric. Tug the tail of the yarn so it's dangling freely on the back side. Flipping the fabric back over, pull the needle out and place your needle a short distance away to make a stitch. Repeat, making sure that the open part of the tip is facing the direction you are going. Embroider around the face, filling the entire hoop with thread. To finish, stick your needle through the fabric, flip it over, and pull out a few inches of yarn from the needle; cut the yarn and remove your needle. Remove the hoop. If using monk's cloth, follow the instructions on page 25 to turn it into a pillow.

Throw an All Saints' Day Party

Let's celebrate the saints! Throw a party to remember and honor the people who came before us. Remember your favorite saints by making big saints' faces, make a photo-booth shrine so people can emulate and show off their favorite saints, and eat foods from the various countries of saints around the world.

Create Big Saints' Faces

* Large circular pieces of cardboard (or cardboard pizza rounds)
* Acrylic paint
* Paintbrushes
* Poster board or cardstock
* Scissors
* Glue

Paint the cardboard circles to be various skin colors. Then cut out poster board and cardstock to make their facial features: noses, lips, eyes, and so on. Paint them and, when dry, glue them onto the cardboard.

Construct a Shrine Niche Photo Booth

* Cardboard box large enough to sit in
* Cardboard pieces
* Tape
* Spray paint
* Acrylic paint
* Paintbrushes
* Box cutter
* Curtain
* Stool
* Glitter, optional

Set up a large box for the shrine. Make a border with cardboard pieces and tape it around the edges of the shrine. Spray-paint the structure, and paint some designs with acrylic paint. Decorate with glitter (to symbolize the glory of heaven) if desired. Hang a curtain in the back of the box. Set it up with a stool for your party guests to take pictures dressed in their saint costumes *or* offer the large saint faces for people to use in their photos.

Make Food for Saints from around the World

Use some food ideas from this book (examples on pp. 72, 90, 96, 102, 170, 199, 202, 204, 214) for your menu. Introduce different saints to your party guests.

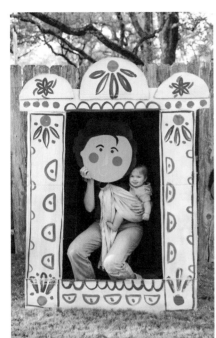

ALL SOULS' DAY

NOVEMBER 2

On All Souls' Day, we honor our deceased loved ones, pray for their souls, and ask them to pray for us. *Memento mori* is an ancient phrase that means "Remember your death," and it has been used in the writings of many saints throughout the ages.

Make an Altar

An *ofrenda* is a traditional altar used in Mexican culture to honor and remember deceased loved ones during the Día de los Muertos (Day of the Dead) celebration. The purpose of an ofrenda is to remember the souls of the deceased by offering food, drink, and other items that they enjoyed in life, and to create a space for family and friends to remember and celebrate their loved ones who have passed away. The ofrenda is typically decorated with bright colors, flowers, candles, and traditional items such as *papel picado* (decorative cut paper), sugar skulls, and *pan de muerto* (bread of the dead). Select a place to set up your ofrenda using a table or altar. Here are some ideas for you to consider while decorating it:

GATHER PICTURES AND MEMENTOS: Collect pictures and mementos of loved ones who have passed away and arrange them on the ofrenda.

INCLUDE FAVORITE ITEMS: Add favorite items of the deceased, such as books, musical instruments, and art. Favorite foods and drinks of the deceased are placed on the ofrenda.

DECORATE WITH MARIGOLDS: Marigolds, also known as *cempasuchil*, are a traditional flower used in Mexican ofrendas. You can use them to decorate the ofrenda or scatter them around the area.

OFFER WATER AND SALT: Place a bowl of water and a bowl of salt on the ofrenda to help the spirits refresh themselves after their journey.

LIGHT CANDLES: Candles are an important part of the ofrenda. Light candles to guide the spirits to the ofrenda and to symbolize hope and faith.

PLAY MUSIC: Play the deceased's favorite music or traditional Mexican music such as mariachi or *ranchera*.

SHARE MEMORIES: Gather with loved ones and share memories and stories of those who have passed away, keeping their memories alive and celebrating their life.

Visit a Cemetery

Go to a cemetery to visit the burial place of a beloved deceased family member, and say a prayer for them.

CHRIST THE KING

The Feast of Christ the King is the last Sunday of the liturgical year before Advent begins. It's a feast to remind us that Jesus is the true King of Peace we long for, who came "to reconcile to himself all things" (Col 1:20), who came "not to be served but to serve" (Mt 20:28). He reigns victorious over all of our sufferings, all war, all governments and authorities. Even more, the kingdom of Christ isn't some far-off reality. We are living in and have access to his kingdom now.

Cook a Feast Fit for a King

To celebrate Christ the King, for dinner make roasted chicken à la king and potatoes. Serve special drinks in fancy goblets.

Make Crowns

You can find instructions for kings crowns on page 52.

Serve Others

> *It will not be so among you, but whoever wishes to be great among you must be your servant, and whoever wishes to be first among you must be your slave, just as the Son of Man came not to be served but to serve and to give his life a ransom for many.*
> —Matthew 20:26–28

Jesus's earthly life taught us the way of the Servant King. For him, these two identities of servant and king go hand in hand. As we build up his kingdom on earth, we are called to the same servant leadership. Think of someone in your life who is the "lowliest." Who has the lowest rank in your office? Who in your friend's circle is often left out or gossiped about? Who in your family is always the scapegoat? Reach out to them today and perform an act of kindness that will build them up.

Make a Viva, Cristo Rey *Banner*

Viva, Cristo Rey means "Long live Christ the King." Bl. Miguel Agustín Pro was a martyr of the Cristeros War for the right to proclaim Jesus as the one true God. In making a banner, we too proclaim Jesus Christ as King of our hearts and our world.

* "*Viva, Cristo Rey* Banner" template
* Canvas banner, 10 x 12 inches (see p. 146 for instructions on making one)
* Different colors of felt
* Fabric scissors
* Felt glue
* Pen
* Scraps of paper
* Tape

Use the template to cut out the letters for *Viva, Cristo Rey* using different colors of felt. Glue them onto the banner with felt glue.

With pen and scrap paper, write at least 3 worries you have about your life or things you hope to happen in the coming year; write each on a separate scrap of paper. Tape them to the back of the banner, and be reminded that Jesus is King and you can trust in him.

ACKNOWLEDGMENTS

My biggest gratitude goes to my husband, who supports me when I take on more than I can handle—such as writing this book just as we had a new baby. Thank you, Paul, for being my biggest advocate and for loving me through my worst moments. And to my daughters, Frances and Lucille, who inspire me and usher me into new horizons of growth. Thank you for making me want to be the best version of myself.

I want to honor the Heart's Home (now known as Con-Solatio) community that I lived with in Brazil, the Brooklyn community that I lived with in New York, and all the friends I made in those eighteen months. You taught me so much about living in the rhythm of the Church, and you all carried me when I was still so young and knew so little about the richness of tradition. I forever carry you in my heart into all that I do and am. Thank you for loving me so well.

Thank you to my parents, Jim and Jennie. None of this would have been possible without you helping me care for the girls and flying in at a moment's notice when I needed more time to work. Thank you for jumping in to help water grass, hang piñatas, and sew tents. Thanks to my mother-in-law, Genny, for baking things for us—we all know that my cookies would be unphotographable.

To Augusta, who encouraged me to say yes when I was ready to say no. Thank you for all of your wisdom, for your creative brain, and for doing this with me. Thank you to Olivia, who said yes to come help before you really knew what you were getting yourself into; thanks for all the late nights crafting and for helping me get my brain organized so that this book was possible. And to Hannah: Thank you for your friendship all these years and for taking on this project that was far more work than you could have known; it would be nothing without your gifts of creating and capturing beauty. A special thanks to my spiritual director, Fr. Michael: You have helped me come to know God to be loving and caring and encouraged me to lean into the mystery of who God is; I am forever grateful. And to all my countless friends who listen to me complain, who commiserate in the exhaustion that is motherhood, who inspire me in your faith and who you are as women—Shannon, Jacqui, Colleen, Marylouise, Elissa, Kristin, Alex, Rakhi, Shannon, Clare, Justina, Marcia, Shannon, Kelly, Steph, Sallie, Brenna, Grace, Lisa, Gillean, Teresa, Taylor, Gaby, Katie, Beth, Liz, Carla, Madison, Michelle, Kelsey, Alison, Kristin, Hayley, and certainly more I have forgotten.

Lastly, a big thanks to the team at Ave Maria Press who was as excited about this project as I was and for helping me to see it beyond what I first imagined. Thank you for reminding me that there was something beautiful here to explore and share with others when I felt like giving up.

APPENDIX: ADDITIONAL READING

Many amazing feast days and saints could not fit on these pages. Here are my favorite books to explore and discover more:

* *Around the Year with the Von Trapp Family* by Maria Von Trapp (Sophia Institute Press, 2018)
* *The Catholic All Year Compendium: Liturgical Living for Real Life* by Kendra Tierney (Ignatius Press, 2018)
* *The Catholic Home: Celebrations and Traditions for Holidays, Feast Days, and Every Day* by Meredith Gould (Image, 2006)
* *Catholic Household Blessings and Prayers* by USCCB (Image, 2012)
* *Come to the Table: A Catholic Passover Seder for Holy Week* by Meredith Gould (Plowshares, 2005)
* *From Saint Hildegard's Kitchen: Foods of Health, Foods of Joy* by Jany Fournier-Rosset (Liguori, 2010)
* *A Saint a Day* by Meredith Hinds (Thomas Nelson, 2021)
* *Saints Around the World* by Meg Hunter-Kilmer (Emmaus Road, 2021)
* *To Light Their Way: A Collection of Prayers and Liturgies for Parents* by Kayla Craig (Tyndale Momentum, 2021)

NOTES

ADVENT

1. Reprinted from *Bless Us, O Lord: A Family Treasury of Mealtime Prayers* by Robert M. Hamma (Notre Dame, IN: Ave Maria Press, 2020).

2. Edward Hays, "St. Nicholas Day Blessing of Candy Canes," *Prayers for the Domestic Church: A Handbook for Worship in the Home* (Notre Dame, IN: Ave Maria Press, 2007), 147.

CHRISTMAS

1. Francis, "Homily of Pope Francis on the Solemnity of the Epiphany of the Lord," The Holy See, January 6, 2019, https://www.vatican.va/content/francesco/en/homilies/2019/documents/papa-francesco _20190106_omelia-epifania.html.

ORDINARY TIME I

1. Commonly attributed to St. Anselm's "Enarration of St. Luke," cited by Prosper Gueranger, *The Liturgical Year*, trans. Laurence Shepherd, 3rd ed. vol. 2, *Christmas* (Worcester: Stanbrook Abbey, 1904), 534, https://hdl. handle.net/2027/hvd.32044105532220.

LENT

1. Francis, *Patris Corde (With a Father's Heart)*, The Holy See, December 8, 2020, sec. 7, https://www. vatican.va/content/francesco/en/apost_letters/documents/papa-francesco-lettera-ap_20201208_patris-corde.html.

2. Fulton J. Sheen, *Life of Christ* (New York: Doubleday, 1977), 10.

HOLY WEEK

1. Michael J. Callaghan, "Litany of Light," in *Holy Week at Home*, Be a Heart, accessed February 20, 2023, https://files.ecatholic.com/15541/documents/2020/4/HolyWeekatHome.pdf?t=1585931577000. Used with permission.

EASTER

1. St. Faustina Kowalska, *Divine Mercy in My Soul: Diary of St. Maria Faustina Kowalska* (Stockbridge, MA: Marian Press, 1987), sec. 687.

2. Kowalska, sec. 299.

3. Kowalska, sec. 48.

4. Kowalska, sec. 1320; see also sec. 1572.

ORDINARY TIME II

1. Ignatius of Loyola, *A Pilgrim's Journey: The Autobiography of Ignatius of Loyola* (San Francisco: Ignatius Press, 2001), 75.

2. "Prayer for Marriage," written by Josh and Stacey Noem.

3. Andre Frossard, *Forget Not Love: The Passion of Maximilian Kolbe*, trans. Cendrine Fontan (San Francisco: Ignatius Press, 1991), 23.

4. Teresa of Calcutta, "Noble Peace Prize Acceptance Speech," transcript of speech delivered at the University of Oslo, Norway, December 10, 1979, https://www.nobelprize.org/prizes/peace/1979/teresa/acceptance-speech/.

5. Teresa of Calcutta, "Nobel Peace Prize Lecture" (lecture, Noble Peace Prize, Oslo, Norway, December 11, 1979), https://www.nobelprize.org/prizes/peace/1979/teresa/lecture/.

6. Jany Fournier-Rosset, *From Saint Hildegard's Kitchen: Foods of Health, Foods of Joy* (Liguori, MO: Liguori Publications, 2010), 7.

7. Sam O'Brien, "Eat Like a Medieval Saint with Her Recipe for 'Cookies of Joy,'" *Atlas Obscura*, September 20, 2021, https://www.atlasobscura.com/articles/medieval-cookie-recipe.

8. Recipe adapted from O'Brien, "Eat Like a Medieval Saint with Her Recipe for 'Cookies of Joy.'"

9. Traditional rhyme for Michaelmas.

10. Thérèse of Lisieux, *The Story of a Soul: The Autobiography of St. Thérèse of Lisieux,* trans. John Clarke (Washington: ICS Publications, 1976), 136.

11. Cuthbert, *Life of St. Francis of Assisi* (London: Longmans, Green, 1925), 32, HathiTrust.

12. Francis of Assisi, "The Prayer before the Crucifix (1205/06)," in *Francis of Assisi: Early Documents*, ed. Regis J. Armstrong, J. Wayne Hellmann, and William J. Short, vol. 1, *The Saint* (Hyde Park, NY: New City Press, 1999), 40.

13. Recipe adapted from "Almond Cookies for St. Francis of Assisi," *St. Anthony Shrine*, accessed February 20, 2023, https://www.stanthony.org/almond-cookies-for-st-francis-of-assisi/.

14. *Francis of Assisi, Early Documents: Vol. 1, The Saint,* Francis of Assisi, Regis J. Armstrong, J. A. Wayne Hellmann, and William J. Short. Published by New City Press, Hyde Park, NY, 1999. Used with permission.

15. John Paul II, "Message of His Holiness Pope John Paul II For the Celebration of the XXX World Day of Peace: Offer Forgiveness and Receive Peace," The Holy See, January 1997, sec. 4, https://www.vatican.va/content/john-paul-ii/en/messages/peace/documents/hf_jp-ii_mes_08121996_xxx-world-day-for-peace.html.

INDEX OF FEAST DAYS

INDEX OF SAINTS

INDEX OF TEMPLATES

ERICA TIGHE CAMPBELL is the owner and artist behind Be A Heart, a popular Christian modern lifestyle brand.

She offers an original collection of textiles, accessories, party goods, fine-art prints, and award-winning calligraphy that models hope and light in the midst of personal and social darkness. The beauty of diversity inspires her artwork.

Campbell earned a bachelor's degree in sociology from DePaul University. She served as a missionary with Con-solatio in Salvador da Bahia, Brazil. She is the author of *Written by Hand* and designed stationery for high-profile events in Los Angeles for many years.

She has been a guest on a number of Catholic podcasts and her work has been featured in *Elle* magazine and *Goop*.

www.beaheart.com
Facebook: www.facebook.com/beaheartdesign
Instagram: @beaheartdesign
Pinterest: @beaheartdesign